# LOOKING TOWARD
# THE PRIESTHOOD

# LOOKING TOWARD THE PRIESTHOOD

The nature, dignity, necessity and signs
of a sacerdotal vocation.

BY

RT. REV. CHARLES HUGO DOYLE

St. Paul Publications
QUEEN OF APOSTLES SEMINARY
DERBY, NEW YORK

*Nihil Obstat*:

> Gall Higgins, O.F.M. Cap.
> *Censor Librorum*

*Imprimatur*:

> ✠ Francis Cardinal Spellman
> Archbishop of New York
> March 28, 1961

LIBRARY OF CONGRESS CATALOG CARD NUMBER: 61-10287
COPYRIGHT, © 1961 BY THE SOCIETY OF ST. PAUL. DERBY, N.Y.
PRINTED IN U.S.A., BY THE SOCIETY OF ST. PAUL, DERBY, N.Y.

# DEDICATION

To the Alumni of St. Augustine's Seminary,
Toronto, Ontario, Canada,
and
to the class of 1929, whose motto was
*Duc In Altum.*

Other Books by
Monsignor Charles Hugo Doyle

*Cana Is Forever*
*Pride — Thief of the Holocaust*
*Guidance in Spiritual Direction*
*Leaven of Holiness*
*Little Steps to Great Holiness*
*Reflections on the Passion*
*Blame No One But Yourself!*
*We Have A Pope*
*The Life of Pope Pius XII*

# PREFACE

Decisions are always hard to make, especially when much is hanging in the balance. Worldly-wise business executives, when faced with the need of making decisions, resort to business conferences. Doctors seek counsel from fellow practitioners by means of consultations. And you ... do you find yourself indecisive about what step to take vocation-wise? You have done well to start reading about the priesthood and consulting experienced writers on the subject. In the following pages you will discover Monsignor Doyle to be a competent and sympathetic guide to help you surmount such hurdles as the tantalizing questions: Can I be happy in the priesthood? Can God really be calling me, unworthy as I know I am? How do I know whether to "go for" the diocesan or religious priesthood? Do I have the requisite qualities of body, mind and character? How can I overcome the opposition of my parents? On each of these topics Monsignor Doyle has devoted "full coverage" and has employed a very readable style.

After reading to the end of the book, then with God's grace take the next logical step toward the priesthood. That is, in the words of Monsignor Doyle..."talk the matter over frankly with your pastor, confessor or spiritual director. Miraculous as was St. Paul's conversion, our Lord made use of a human guide to direct him into the priesthood. God taught Ananias what to say to St. Paul, and so, God may enlighten your pastor, confessor or spiritual director regarding your vocation."

# CONTENTS

## CHAPTER ONE

# OUR ENEMY — THE WORLD

After the death of Abderman, Calif of Cordova, the following paper was found in his own handwriting: "Fifty years have elapsed since I became Calif. I have possessed riches, honors, pleasures, friends; in short, everything that man can desire in this world. I have reckoned up the days in which I could say I was really happy; and they amount to fourteen."

The great pursuit of man is after happiness: it is the first and the strongest desire of his nature. In every stage of life he searches for it as for a great and elusive treasure; courts it under a thousand different shapes, and, although perpetually disappointed, still persists, runs after, and inquires for it anew.

He is told by one person to seek it among the gay and useless pleasures of life, in scenes of mirth and merriment, where happiness ever presides, and is ever to be known by the joy and laughter which emanates from the theater, the night-club or the dance-hall.

Another person, with a graver aspect, points out that happiness dwells in the homes pride and extravagance have erected; that happiness lives only in company with the great, in the midst of much pomp and outward state; that amidst great luxury and expensive furniture and appointments, happiness is sure to be found.

The miser, on the other hand, is certain to tell him that if he would not be disappointed in his search for happiness, he must look into the plain and thrifty domicile of the prudent man, who knows and values the importance of money, and cautiously lays it up against an evil hour, that it is in keeping money together — *having* and *holding* it fast to him and his heirs forever — that forms happiness.

The epicure maintains that there is nothing better in this world than that a man should eat and drink, and rejoice in his works, and make his soul enjoy good in his labor, for that is his portion. To rescue him from this brutal experiment, ambition takes him by the hand and carries him into the world, shows him all the kingdoms of the earth and the glory of them, points out the many ways of advancing his fortune, and raising himself to honor; lays before his eyes all the charms and bewitching temptations of power, and asks if there can be any happiness in this world like that of being caressed, courted, flattered and followed.

Somewhere in life, the searcher for happiness is sure to be confronted by the philosopher who tells him that if he is in search of happiness, he is on the wrong track altogether; that this elusive good has long been banished by noise and tumults, and has fled into solitude from all the commerce of the world; and, in a word, if he would find happiness at all, he must leave this busy and intriguing scene, and go back to that peaceful scene of retirement and books, from which he at first departed.

In this circle, too often does man run, trying all experiments, and generally, at last, he sits down weary and disillusioned, in utter despair of ever accomplishing what he wants or knowing in what to place his trust after so many will-o'-the-wisp sorties and after so many disappointments. He is puzzled as to where to lay the blame — upon the incapacity of his nature or the insufficiency of the enjoyments themselves.

In re-reading what I have written above, I am convinced more than ever that this is no uncommon picture of the disappointments and disillusionments of human life, but the true picture of how pleasure and enjoyments elude us in every stage of life. Far be it from me, on the other hand, to deny the reality of pleasures or dispute the existence of them any more than I would deny the reality of pain; yet I must observe that there is a plain distinction to be made between pleasure and happiness. Yet I do maintain that while there can be no happiness without pleasure, the reverse of the proposition will not hold true. We are so made, that from the common gratifications of our appetites and the impressions of a thousand objects, we snatch the one, like a transient gleam, without being suffered to taste the other, and enjoy the perpetual sunshine and fair weather which constantly attend it. This, I contend, is to be found only in religion.

Religion consists in a knowledge of God and a life corresponding to the Will of God: our Lord taught: "This is eternal life, that they may know Thee, the only true God, and Jesus Christ, Whom Thou hast sent" (John 17:3); that is to say, the knowledge of God brings man to eternal happiness. But along with this must go the fulfilling of the Will of God through the keeping of the commandments, for, as the Saviour Himself said to the rich young man: "If thou wilt enter into life, keep the commandments" (Matt. 19:17). You see, it is also true that he who desires to be happy must strive to be like to God. Man becomes like God when all his thoughts and actions resemble the divine thoughts and actions. The commandments of God are a mirror, in which we recognize whether our actions are like or unlike those of God.

Never did the busy brain of a lean and hectic chemist search for the philosopher's stone with more pains and ardour than did Solomon search after happiness. He was one of the wisest inquirers into nature. He had tried all her powers and capacities, and, after a thousand vain speculations and vile experiments, affirmed at length that it lay hidden in not one thing he tried. Like the chemist's projections, all had ended in vapors and smoke, or what was worse, in vanity and vexation of spirit. The conclusion of the whole matter was this — that he advised that every man who would be happy *must fear God and keep His commandments.* (Eccles 12:13).

Pleasures sought, or proposed, that are in direct opposition to the Commandments of God may promise pleasure or profit, but it is the old, old story of Eve's deception repeated over and over again. Delila's smile and favors

were but bitter memories to the blind Samson. The taste
of the bait matters little to the fish when it feels the pain
of the hook.

If some think that any happiness or pleasure
may be enjoyed through, and by, the commission of
thought, words, actions or omission contrary to the Commandments of God, let them re-read the following bitter
confession of one who had drained the cup of illicit pleasures to the very dregs only to find such potions just left
him "arrogant and depressed, weary and restless."

St. Augustine's youthful search for pleasure led to his
soul-stirring *Confessions*. With tears streaming down his
face, he spoke thus to his God: "Loveliness, happy and
abiding, I collect myself out of that broken state in which
my being was torn asunder because I turned away from
Thee and wasted myself upon the many; for even in my
youth I burned for all the satisfactions of hell, and I sank
even to the animal in a succession of dark lusts. My one
delight was to love and to be loved. But in this I did not
keep the measure of mind to mind, which is the luminous
love of friendship; but from the muddy concupiscence of
the flesh and the hot imagination of puberty, mists streamed
up to becloud and darken my heart so that I could not
distinguish the white light of love from the fog of lust. Both
love and lust boiled within me, and swept my youthful
immaturity over the precipice of evil desires to leave me
half-drowned in a whirlpool of abominable sins; I had
grown deaf from the clanging of the chain of my mortality,
the punishment of the pride of my soul: I departed further
from You and You left me to myself: and I was tossed

about and wasted and poured out and boiling over in my sins: and You were silent, O my late-won Joy. You were silent and I, arrogant and depressed, weary and restless, wandered further from You into more and more sins which could bear no fruit save sorrows . . . Nor did I escape Your scourges. No mortal can. You were always by me, mercifully hard upon me, and besprinkling all my illicit pleasures with certain elements of bitterness, to draw me on to seek pleasures in which no bitterness should be. And where was I to find such pleasures save in You, O Lord."

We stated earlier that he who desires happiness must have religion, and that religion consists in the knowledge of God and a life corresponding to the Will of God, but let me say here that religion is not a matter of feeling: it is a matter of the will and of action, and consists in following the principles that God has laid down. Mere knowledge does not constitute religion, else the devil would have religion; the service of God is necessarily included in it. We do not call a man a tennis player or baseball player because he knows the rules and nature of the game; playing the part is also required.

The greatest folly of man is, that, in coming from the Hand of God and being placed in this world to be tested as to his worthiness for eternal happiness in heaven, he becomes so attached to the world that he forgets the end of his creation. Man was created to give glory to God, to know, love and serve Him in this life with his whole heart, soul and mind, and to be happy with Him in heaven for all eternity.

Christ revealed to man a truth of paramount importance. Hear Him as He says: "I give testimony of the world that the works thereof are evil" (John 7:7). Now, what possible reason could have existed for such a forthright warning had the *evil* of these *works* been already known to mankind. There are millions who, from ignorance of this truth, place implicit confidence in the world, worship it, cleave to it, and every day of their lives become more devoted to its service. Would God, I could disclose to all the artful devices and the many traps it lays for us, so that we might reach that high state St. Paul achieved when he wrote: "The world is crucified to me" (Gal. 6:14). Perhaps it is too much to hope that we could be other Pauls, yet, at least we could resolve not to love the world, not to be on such friendly terms with it, not to give it our confidence.

This may be initiated only if we first confess the strong inclination we feel to serve the world. But what is that quality in the world which disposes and inclines us to serve it? No doubt it is the promises it offers, all so rich, so munificent, and in such perfect harmony with our taste. This must be it. The world promises us pleasures, it promises us riches, it promises us honors, these advantages which mortals naturally covet, which men pursue with the desperate fondness of the silly insect for the flame of the candle, the very things we know to have ruined multitudes.

How is it that our eyes are not open to detect the imposture? You see, this same wondrous condescension ought to be the very thing to furnish us with clear, certain and infallible evidence of the world's hereby declaring itself to be a traitor. Every traitor manages to creep into people's favor by offering them something agreeable to the senses. Cain, for instance, betrayed Abel by proposing to him a ramble into the woods: "Let us go forth abroad" (Gen. 4:8). Delila betrayed Samson by inviting to a fond endearment. Tryphon betrayed Jonathan by giving him, at first, an honorable reception (1 Mach. 12). St. John Chrysostom wisely remarks: "The chief business of a deceiver is to offer first what pleases, that he may inflict afterwards what pains."

Therefore, as long as the world so indulgently panders to our natural and even our corrupt and inordinate desires, we are not quite certain that it is not treating us fairly and handsomely. Careful scrutiny, however, will demonstrate that they are all mere illusions, apparent gifts, but in reality, real injuries.

True, the votaries of the world have their pleasures, but ask Augustine, the Saint, how Augustine, the sinner, re-acted to them. The votaries of the world have their riches but these same riches frequently condemn them to a life of constant disquietude. Come with me in spirit to a meeting of nine of the world's most successful business men in the Edgewater Beach Hotel in Chicago, held there in 1923. Those present were Samuel Insul, president of the largest utilities company; Charles Schwab, president of the still largest corporation, 200 times a millionaire; Harold Hopson, president of the largest gas company; Arthur Cutten, greatest wheat speculator; Richard Whitney, president of the New York Stock Exchange; Albert Fall, member of the President's cabinet; Jesse Livermore, the greatest speculator on Wall Street; Ivan Krueger, the head of the greatest monopoly; Leon Fraser, president of the Bank of International Settlements.

But see what happened to these same nine men within the following twenty-five years:

> 3 died in bankruptcy,
>
> 1 lost his mind,
>
> 2 went to prison,
>
> 3 committed suicide.

All knew how to make money. Not one of them knew how to live!

The world offers its votaries pleasures from honors but how empty most of them really are! Ask Queen Elizabeth, the First, on her death-bed, what good the fact that a nation called her "Queen" did, in that moment, to soothe and satisfy her. With ten thousand gowns in her wardrobe and an empire at her feet, she tossed on her bed, crying out in vain, "Millions in money for an inch of time."

Ask Cardinal Wolsey, en route to prison, if he had found comfort in the fact that he had held next to the highest offices in Church and State. When accused of treason by the king he served more faithfully than he did his God, he was forced to cry out: "Had I but served my God with half the zeal I served my king, He would not in mine age have left me naked to mine enemies." [1]

The cruelty of the world to its votaries is notorious. A news story came out of Chicago two years ago. An actress, once the pride and boast of Broadway, called by theatre

---

(1) Shakespeare, King Henry VIII, Act III, Scene 2.

critics of her day: "The Most Beautiful Girl on Broadway", jumped from a window to her death.

In the twenty-five years from the time she was the toast of the theatre-set, her beauty had faded and gone, she was alone, jobless, forgotten, and penniless, so she hurled herself from a window, leaving a cryptic note saying she had "no wish to live because the world has forgotten me."

It is a notable fact that it is only those who have spoken and written against the traitorous nature of worldliness, those who have turned their backs upon the world, who are today remembered and honored. As Holy Scripture says: "The memory of the just is with praises" (Prov. 10:7). The world has known more than one Alexius, whom it constantly remembers; a man who exposed it to open scorn by forsaking his parental roof more than a thousand years ago. It remembers more than one Bernard, who despised its pleasures; more than one Francis, who despised its riches; more than one Norbert who, sooner than gain its honors, submitted to the most intolerable hardships. What homes do you recall that have a picture or statue of Queen Elizabeth I in an honored place? But recall that in millions of churches, chapels and homes in the four corners of the earth, the sweet, kind, lovely face of the Little Flower of Jesus, St. Thérèse, looks down benignly upon her clients; and each new generation to the end of the world will honor and applaud, lauding her and all the other saintly men, women and children who have turned their backs on the world and its false maxims, with every high mark and tribute of respect.

That golden image which Nabuchodonosor erected to represent his supreme majesty is everywhere famous. Having assembled around it the different states of his empire, both civil and military, he commanded that, at the first sound of a great variety of musical instruments, all were to fall down and worship it. In this vast assembly only three young men were to be found who dared to despise this royal edict. Protesting openly against such a ceremony, and expressing a detestation of such a worship, they would sooner go into a fiery furnace, hot as hell-fire, than comply. "Be it known to thee, O king, that we will not worship thy gods, nor adore the golden statue which thou hast set up." (Dan. 3:18). Now, who, pray, were the persons whom this same king at last came to honor? Whom did he advance? Whom did he make his favorites? Was it they who were so ready to fall down and pay him such vile adoration? Most assuredly not. But the three young men who had despised him — these were the persons prominently selected for great honors. For, from their not having felt the fires into which they had been cast, the king knew them to be in favor with God, and by a new edict promoted them to a dignity as lofty as could be desired. "After he saw them standing up and nobly erect, he had them proclaimed, and crowned them; and this he did for no other reason," and here let St. Chrysostom supply the reason "for no other reason than because they had despised him."

Now, this is precisely what the world is imitating every day before our eyes. Those who are impatient to bow themselves before its image, it afterwards neglects. While those who, so far from complying with its worship, would rather enter the furnace, however hot, of pain, disgrace, persecution, or withdrawal from worldly pursuits, it honors. How great, therefore, must be the error of supposing that the world, for the best services one can render it, will, under any circumstances, repay you in thanks and favors. Indeed, it will always prove itself faithless, always treacherous, always ungrateful. Withdraw from it in the service of Christ and it will honor you.

To serve the world! Oh! the imposition of heavy laws we must then submit to, and the oppressive burdens we will have to bear, far more oppressive than any to be borne in the service of Christ. Unquestionably, Christ does impose strict laws on His servants; they must submit and humble themselves, they must deny themselves, they must forgive and forbear, but we are sure that when Christ demands such things of man, He will give him, together with His demands, strength to perform them. He will assist his servants as he did Stephen, exposed to a hurricane of stones. He will strengthen him as He did Anthony, abandoned to a mutitude of devils. The servant of God in the priesthood has no grounds for complaint, for, as St. Leo most excellently observes: "He, Who presents us with His assistance, had a good right to urge upon us His demands."

The rest of this work will avail nothing if we are not convinced that an inordinate love of the world and worldly pursuits are great evils. True, we must live in the world, but we must not allow the world to take possession of our souls. A ship floats on water and all is well, but if the water enters the ship in great quantities, she sinks.

Someone has said that man could learn to be cautious

of the world by watching the birds. Have you ever noticed how, when they must drop to the earth for food or water, they are constantly on guard, and as soon as their mission is accomplished they hasten to safety above the earth? They are suspicious, they are fearful as to what might happen to them if they tarry longer than necessary.

Let us never forget that Christ, the Son of God, came to be our *way* and our *light* to eternity. He had encountered Satan on a mountain-top, and He Himself heard Satan offer Him "all the kingdoms of the world and the glory of them if He would but fall down and adore him" (Matth. 4:8-9). And Christ's answer must ever be etched on our hearts: "Begone, Satan! For it is written: 'The Lord thy God shalt thou adore, and Him only shalt thou serve.'" (Matth. 4:10). If Satan would tempt Christ with worldliness, can any of us hope to escape similar temptation? The trouble with most of us is that we succumb to these temptations and look for the "father of lies" to keep his promises.

Is it any wonder, then, that fresh from His ordeal with Satan, the Saviour should mount another mountain and issue His most famous principles by which we must be guided in this world? Hear our Lord say:

1. Blessed are the poor in spirit: for theirs is the Kingdom of Heaven.
2. Blessed are the meek: for they shall possess the land.
3. Blessed are they that mourn: for they shall be comforted.
4. Blessed are they that hunger and thirst after justice: for they shall have their fill.

5. Blessed are the merciful: for they shall obtain mercy.
6. Blessed are the clean of heart: for they shall see God.
7. Blessed are the peacemakers: for they shall be called the children of God.
8. Blessed are they that suffer persecution for justice sake: for theirs is the Kingdom of Heaven.

Compare the foregoing with the code of conduct taught and practiced by the world. The world has its own maxims and declares as fools those whom Christ declares as blessed. Hear the world proclaim:

1. Riches constitute the greatest happiness, poverty is the greatest misery. If a man has anything at all he must make a show of it. It pays to advertise. "Money is life to us wretched mortals," said Hesodius.
2. When you are soft, people take advantage of you. Don't let people walk all over you. Fight for your rights!
3. Happy is the man who is free from care and sorrow.
4. If you don't look after yourself, who will? Beat the other fellow to the punch.
5. Never give a man a chance to make the same mistake twice.
6. Wine, women and song. Live it up! You're only young once!
7. Fight your own battles. Get there first with the most. Hit first, and ask questions afterwards.
8. You've got to live, so a little compromise never hurt anyone.

Is it any wonder then that St. Paul could say in all truth: "The wisdom of this world is foolishness with God." (1. Cor. 3:19).

So impressed was St. John with the dangers arising from worldliness that he mentions it no less than fifty-one times in his inspired writings. Hear him once again saying: "Love not the world, nor the things that are in the world. If any man love the world, the charity of the Father is not in him." (1 John 2: 15)

St. Paul took up the cause, and he pleaded with his followers: "Be not conformed to this world." (Rom. 12:2). Would to God that we could learn the true dangers of worldliness and be able to say with St. Paul: "The world is crucified to me, and I to the world." (Gal. 6:14).

The great St. Augustine poses a question that demands an answer from each one of us: "Which dost thou prefer, to love the world and go into perdition, or to love Christ and enter into everlasting life?" Ever so quickly, he adds: "If thou wouldst not be an enemy of God, be an enemy of the world."

Here it might be well to summarize in what ways the love of the world is opposed to the love of God:

1. The love of the world consists in loving, above all, money or gratification of one's appetite, or earthly honors, or anything else in the world, instead of giving the first place to God.

2. Through love of the world we incur the loss of sanctifying grace, and eternal felicity.

3. The love of the world blinds the soul of man and leads him away from God.

4. The love of the world destroys interior peace, and makes men fear death greatly.

5. The love of the world gives rise to hatred of God and of His servants.

6. The love of the world causes death. Perhaps we should stop here and resolve to choose God for our Friend above all other things, so that when others forsake us, He will not abandon us.

If man is always by nature in pursuit of happiness, and if worldliness, as we have seen, cannot give man lasting happiness, then what can? The answer is simple: *cultivate piety* (*godliness*), which, as St. Paul says, "Is profitable to all things, having the promise of the life that *now* is and of that which is to come." (1 Tim. 4:8). Peace of soul, the joy of a good conscience, the happiness of union with God, of growing in His love, of effecting a closer intimacy with Christ — such are a few of the rewards which, along with the comforting hope of eternal life, God dispenses even now to His faithful servants in the midst of their trials.

How then, are we to attain eternal happiness?

1. We must strive to know God by means of faith in the truths He has revealed to us.

2. We must fulfill the Will of God by keeping His commandments.

3. We must avail ourselves of graces; chief sources of which are Holy Mass, the Sacraments and prayer.

It is a sad thing to say, but modern young men have such a thirst for pleasure that its prompt acquisition seems to be their most important, goal. Materialism, an inordinate love of material things, and worldliness, an inordinate

love of worldly pleasures, are the two great causes of the
dearth of vocations to the priesthood today. Both these
evils bespeak a childish spirit carried into teen-age and
youth. The child lives in the present hour; today is
everything to him. The holiday promised for a much later
date is no holiday at all: it must be either now or never.
Natural in the child, and therefore pardonable, this spirit
when carried on into teen-age, youth or manhood, of course,
is reprehensible. The most distinct illustration given us of
this is the case of Esau.

Esau came from hunting worn and hungry; the only
means of procuring the tempting serving of his brother's
pottage was the sacrifice of his father's blessing, which,
in those ages, carried with it a substantial advantage. But
that birthright could be enjoyed only after *years;* the
pottage was *present,* near and certain; therefore he sacrificed
the future and higher blessings for a present and lower
pleasure. For this reason, Esau is the Bible type of worldliness, he is called in Scripture "a profane," (Heb. 12:16)
that is, not distinctly a vicious person, but a secular or
worldy one, an overgrown child, impetuous, inconsistent not
without gleams of generosity and kindness, but over-
accustomed to immediate gratification.

If there is a dearth of vocations to the priesthood,
both diocesan and religious, and to the brotherhoods today,
it just could be that modern youth is suffering from an
overdose of Esauism. There is little doubt in my mind
that, being over-accustomed to immediate gratification,
modern youth is inclined to prefer a lesser, lower, *present*
pleasure than wait for a higher, *future* pleasure that entails

blessings of a hundred-fold in this life and eternal happiness in the next. This is truly worldliness at its worst.

Our Blessed Lord never pointed out an evil while He dwelt on this earth, without the Holy Ghost having prescribed an antidote. And what is the antidote for worldliness? St. John, the Evangelist, was inspired by the Holy Ghost to write: "And this is the victory which overcometh the world, our faith." (1. John, 5:4).

## CHAPTER TWO

## OVERCOMING THE WORLD

One day when our Lord was on this earth He came to the district of Judea beyond the Jordan, where a young man came to Him to ask a very important question.

"Good Master," said the youth, "what good work shall I do to have eternal life?"

Our Lord said to him: "Why dost thou ask Me about what is good? One there is Who is good, that is God. But if thou wilt enter into life, keep the commandments."

"Which?" asked the young man.

And Jesus said:

"Thou shalt not kill,
Thou shalt not commit adultery,
Thou shalt not steal,
Thou shalt not bear fa'se witness,
Honor thy father and mother, and
Thou shalt love thy neighbor as thyself."

The young man said to our Lord: "All these I have kept; what is yet wanting to me?"

"If thou will be perfect, go, sell what thou hast, and give it to the poor, and thou shalt have treasure in heaven; and come, follow Me."

And then St. Matthew pens the saddest words in all Holy Scripture: "But when the young man heard the saying, he went away sad, for he had great possessions."

It is noteworthy that our Lord said: "If thou *wilt*." You see, this was not a *command* to the rich young man, but rather a *counsel*. However, it is incredible that the youth was not moved by the ring of authority in the Master's words. Something held him back. What was it? His love for his earthly possessions. We can be nearly certain of this, since, when the young man walked sadly away from Christ, the Redeemer turned to His disciples and said: "Amen, I say to you, with difficulty will a rich man enter the Kingdom of heaven." St. Bonaventure, explaining this statement of Christ's, says: "Cupidity is the root of all evil since of it is born ambition, gluttony and the rest of the vices."

Who cou'd ever estimate the number of persons who were as rich as the young man in the Gospel, persons to whom the world held out the most enticing promises, yet, who, upon hearing the words our Lord addressed to the young man, left all things to follow Christ? St. Anthony, hearing those words of Christ read at Mass, left all things and followed the Master. St. Prosper of Regium, who was afterwards a Bishop, did the same, in the time of St. Leo.

Deservedly, St. Bernard says: "These are the words which in all the world have persuaded men to a contempt of the world and to voluntary poverty. They are the words which fill the cloisters with monks, the deserts with anchorites. These, I say, are the words which spoil Egypt, and strip it of the best of its goods. This is the living and effectual word, converting souls, by the happy emulations of sanctity, and the faithful promise of truth."

The strength of the attractiveness of worldly goods and honors is patent. It takes a greater force to overcome these; and the only force that can do this is a strong *faith*. "And this is the victory, which overcometh the world, our faith." (1 John 5:4).

On the heels of the rejected invitation to higher perfection, our Lord spoke of the rewards of those who make sacrifices to follow Him. It all happened this way. St. Peter, upon seeing the young man walk slowly away from our Lord, turned to the Master and said: "Behold, we have left all and followed Thee; what then shall we have?" What Peter actually said, if translated into present-day language was: "What are we going to get for having left all things to follow You?"

Who else among the Apostles would have been so naive as Peter was in putting such a blunt question to our Lord? The impetuous Peter usually said what was on his mind, and here he wanted to know what he and the others who had left their families, friends, and worldly goods would receive as recompense. To the Son of God Who had given up the glories of heaven to become Man, the combined sacrifices of the Apostles must have seemed shabby indeed, but with the most wonderful display of empathy, Christ looked beyond the blunt question and saw what St. Gregory saw in St. Peter's poorly framed words: "He has forsaken

much who has left the desire of having." St. Augustine seemed to justify Peter's thinking he had given up a great deal
when he walked away from his boat and fish-nets to follow
Christ, for he comments: "Peter left not only what he had,
*but what he wished to have.* For what poor person is there
who is not puffed up by worldly hopes? Who does not
daily desire to increase his possessions? That cupidity was
cut off. Peter left the whole world, and Peter received the
things."

Softly, without a trace of irritation, our Blessed Lord
made a reply that has touched the hearts of hundreds of
thousands of young men and women down through the dim
vista of the centuries: "Amen, I say to you that you who
have followed Me, in the regeneration when the Son of Man
shall sit on the throne of His glory, shall also sit on twelve
thrones, judging the twelve tribes of Israel. *And everyone
who has left house, or brothers, or sisters, or father, or mother, or wife, or children, or lands, for My Name's sake,
shall receive a hundredfold, and shall possess life everlasting.*" (Matth. 19:29).

It was faith in those very words of the Son of God
Himself that has raised up a noble priesthood and peopled
our monasteries, convents and seminaries in the past, and
if they are prayerfully studied by young men and women
in the universe today, they will once again drown out the
clarion call of the world; and thousands of sorely needed
priests, brothers and sisters will fill the emptying ranks.
It takes great faith to surrender worldly goods, pleasures
and honors in this life, and to believe that for so doing,
other and greater rewards will be forthcoming in this life

and the next, but "this is the victory which overcometh the world, our faith."

Let us examine carefully the things promised to those who forsake the world as the Apostles did. First, in response to Peter's question: "Behold, we have left all things and followed Thee; what then shall we have?" our Lord replied: "Amen, I say to you that you who have followed Me, in the regeneration when the Son of Man shall sit upon the throne of His glory, shall also sit on twelve thrones, judging the twelve tribes of Israel." (Matth. 19:28).

While some like Richard Victor think that this *sitting in judgment* was a special reward promised to the Apostles alone because they were Christ's first followers, others seem to think that these promises hold good for the followers of the Apostles, such as religious, who, leaving all things to preach the Gospel, come nearest to Christ and His Apostles.

As to the number *twelve*, a definite number is placed here for an indefinite one, that is to say, the word *twelve* stands for *all*. Thus, when Nazianzen shows that it is the privilege of monks to sit on thrones, in as much as those who have done equal labor with the Apostles will deserve equal honors with them, St. Augustine gives proof that he was in agreement with him when he says: "For if there were to be twelve thrones only, Paul, the thirteenth Apostle, would have no throne; and he would not be able to judge, who said nevertheless, that he should judge not men only, but even angels. Not only, then, those twelve, and the Apostle Paul, but as many as shall judge pertain to the twelve thrones, on account of the general signification." (In Ps. 87).

St. Bernard sanctions this interpretation too: "Altogether just is the retribution, that they who here for Christ's sake have forsaken the glory of human majesty, should be glorified by Christ and sit with Him in an especial manner as judges . . . We must understand, therefore, that all who, after the example of the Apostles, have left all things and followed Christ, shall come as judges with Him, even as all men shall be judged; for by the number twelve, in Scripture, totality is often understood; by the twelve thrones of the Apostles the entire number of all who judge, and by the twelve tribes of Israel the entire number of those who are to be judged is shown." (Tract. cont. retrahent. a Relig. chaps. 6 and 7).

St. Gregory, likewise, comments that those who followed the Apostles in poverty shall sit on special thrones with lofty judicial power, for as he says: "The more they were despised in this world through their great humility, so much the more, when they receive their thrones, do they grow in the height of power." (Moral. 26:20).

What a wondrous victory is that faith which makes people forsake worldly goods, worldly honors and pleasurable pursuits to follow Christ, believing the infallible words of the Son of God Himself that those who follow Him shall have especial honor and glory in heaven. Faith in Christ's promises in this instance implies:

1. The security of those who are poor for the Gospel's sake.

2. The privilege of judging.

3. Dignity and eminence over others.

4. The nearest place to Christ and a most perfect union with Him.

5. A principality of grace, happiness and glory. Inasmuch as they are princes of the Kingdom of heaven, they should have the right of judging, and of admitting into it those who are worthy, and excluding the unworthy.

But there was even *more* promised those who accepted Christ's invitation: "And everyone who has left house or brothers, or sisters, or father, or mother, or wife, or children, or lands, for My name's sake, shall receive a hundredfold, and shall possess life everlasting." So spoke the Son of God.

The above sentence intrigued St. Jerome. Its doctrine consoled and encouraged him; its construction challenged him. He became convinced that in the several clauses of this sentence the disjunctive conjunction, *or*, is put there because our Lord is not speaking now of those who left *everything* to follow Him, but of those who only left *some* things for His sake and the Gospel's.

And that *hundredfold* demands special consideration, too. A hundredfold here means *many times more*; a definite number being put for an indefinite number, in order that the vast magnitude of the compensation might be signified.

There are several interpretations of the promises our Lord announced for those who accepted His invitation to the priesthood and to the religious life. St. Jerome and the Venerable Bede took the *hundredfold* to apply, not to temporal, but to spiritual goods, such as peace, joy, divine consolations, and all other gifts and graces with which God comforts them, and which He heaps upon them. These things surpass all earthly goods and joys, far more than a hundred exceeds unity.

But, because St. Mark particularly explains a *hundred times as many,* by adding houses, brethren, sisters, mothers, children and lands — Origen, Theophylact and Cassian explain the hundredfold thus — that the man who forsakes his possessions and friends for Christ's sake, shall find that Christ will take care that he has a hundred, that is, very many others, who will give him the love and help of brothers, wives, and mothers, with far more exceeding sweetness and charity, so that it shall not seem that he has lost his own possessions, but has only laid them down, and in Christ's providence, has multiplied them with compound interest.

Since spiritual affections are sweeter than natural ones, anyone who has left one home for Christ will find a hundred and more homes of pious people open and ready to receive him with love and gladness. A person who has left one house of his father for Christ finds a hundred, not houses, but monasteries, colleges, seminaries and rectories to receive him with paternal kindness. So also, he who has left one field for Christ will find a hundred fields of worshippers of Christ by which he may be nourished, and that without labor or toil, whereas he would have had to cultivate his own field.

In like manner, for one brother forsaken there will be very many Christians who will cherish him with fraternal love, and cleave to him more sweetly with spiritual attachment. For one sister, very many maidens will chastely love him, and attend to his wants like a brother. Instead of one father, very many elders will cherish him as a son. For one mother, very many matrons will supply his necessities with maternal care. In place of a single son or daughter, innumerable children will revere him as a father, and hang upon his sound doctrine and counsels, and from whom he will derive greater pleasure than he could from his own children.

As if the hundredfold reward on this earth were not adequate, our Lord added that those who have left house, or brothers, or sisters, or father, or mother, or wife, or children, or lands for His name's sake *"shall possess life everlasting."* This to me, is the most wonderful reward imaginable — to be heirs of God, and joint heirs with Christ in an eternity of bliss. How could any thinking person hear those words of our Lord and ponder over them, and then refuse to accept His invitation to follow Him in the priesthood and religious life, preferring instead some purely worldly pursuit? It is incredible!

Imagine, a reward or compensation for the acceptance of an invitation from One Who has the right to command, that includes not only a hundredfold more than what is given up to follow Him, but every honor, all riches, all glory, all sweetness, all delights, all joys; in a word, all good things, but most of all, even God Himself. Well could St. Augustine say: "The rewards which follow are such, that, whilst he who has conquered receives, and he who gives, loses nothing." (de Synub. and Catechum, Bk. 2). Now, while it is true that all who keep the commandments shall inherit eternal life, those who forsake all to follow Christ in the priesthood and religious life shall possess eternal life in a fuller and more glorious way.

Let no man deny that it takes faith, a strong faith, to forsake present worldly allurements, pleasures and honors in the firm belief, that in so doing to follow Christ, present and future rewards will surpass anything we have given up. In so believing, in taking God at His word, such a person hopes; by hoping he invokes; by invoking he loves Christ, and therefore is strengthened by the grace of Christ to despise the world; and by despising it, he overcomes it. Now, perhaps, you can better understand what St. John meant when he penned these inspired words: "And this is the victory which overcometh the world, our faith." (1. John 5:4).

Take this little book with you to church some afternoon or evening and open it to this chapter. Pray earnestly for light from the Holy Ghost, and then sit in the presence of our Lord and let your imagination place you in the crowd where the rich young man approaches our Lord and asks his now famous questions regarding salvation and perfection. Use your intelligence to understand each word of Christ's reply to Peter, and then prayerfully ponder over the promises made to those who forsake the world to follow Christ — *a hundred-fold in this life and eternal life in the next*. Ask yourse'f if there is any earthly career that offers so much for so little? End this colloquy with your Eucharistic King by pleading for that sort of faith which will move you to take Him at His word; and then offer yourself to Him to do with you whatever He wishes.

## CHAPTER THREE

## AN HONOR BEYOND ALL HONORS

Imagine if you can what it would be like to come home one day to find a telegram from the President of the United States requesting you to come at your earliest convenience to the White House on a very important matter of business. Imagine further, that, after being received by the President in his office, he proceeds to ask you to accept an appointment with ambassadorial rank as his personal representative to a foreign government. Doubtless, your joy would be boundless and your parents and friends would shower you with congratulations for being asked to assume such an important post. You would feel yourself to be one of the most distinguished and honored persons in the whole nation.

Those who are called to the Catholic priesthood are called to an honor greater than that conferred by any worldly leader, be he King or President. They become, thereby, the ambassadors of God Himself. "For Christ therefore we are ambassadors, God as it were exhorting by us." (2 Cor. 5:20). A priest, therefore, is a minister destined by God to be a public ambassador of the whole Church, to honor God, to obtain His graces for all the faithful. But this will be meaningless unless and until we consider the importance of religion in life.

Life, for the vast majority of men and women, consists in loving and being loved, founding a home and raising a family. To accomplish this it is essential that they make a living as self-employed individuals or find the means in one of the many professions such as law, medicine or teaching, while for others it involves studying, writing, painting, military or public service, such as in the armed forces, or as policemen, firemen, government workers or politicians. To not a few, life is simply a social whirl made up of dancing, travel or sports.

With one or two exceptions, the above listed means of making a livelihood are all praiseworthy, but we would be less than realistic if we did not remark that in trying to be successful in any of the above vocations and avocations, there is danger of becoming so engrossed in material things that one neglects the spiritual. This certainly was Cardinal Wolsey's regret when he fell into disfavor with Henry VIII, for, as we have already noted, he said: "Had I but served my God, with half the zeal I served my king, He would not have left me naked to mine enemies."

We can never afford to forget the primary end of man. Why was man created? For the answer, let us go directly to the word of God. In the Book of Isaias we read that God says of man: "I have created him for My glory, I have formed him and made him." (43:7). Since God made man, he belongs to God, and God can require of him what He wills. And what does God ask of man? Again, let us turn to the inspired Scriptures and read these words: "What doth the Lord thy God require of thee, but that thou fear the Lord thy God, and walk in His ways, and love Him and serve the Lord thy God with all thy heart and with all thy soul." (Deut. 10:12).

When God in His goodness singled us out to be the recipients of Baptism, He conferred upon us, through Sanctifying Grace, the inestimable gift of being made capable of the Beatific Vision by the Divine Life of Grace. Along with Sanctifying Grace, God infused into our souls, much as cream is shot into a cream-puff, the three theological virtues of Faith, Hope and Charity. By Faith, He made it possible for us to know Him as He really is; by Hope, to await with confidence the fulfillment of His promises; by Charity, to love Him as He deserves to be loved, that is, for Himself, and above all things.

Even with these great gifts, it would still be impossible for us by our natural habits and powers to direct our lives as we should. And so, besides the Gifts of Divine Life and the infused theological virtues of Faith, Hope and Charity, God has also given us the infused moral virtues and the Gifts of the Holy Ghost. The infused moral virtues are habits put into our souls by God to make our good actions worthy of heaven; and the Gifts of the Holy Ghost make our souls receptive to the enlightenment and direction of the Holy Ghost.

It is certain from the Council of Trent that at the very moment of our baptism, we receive the infused virtues of

Faith, Hope and Charity. The common doctrine confirmed by the Catechism of the Council of Trent is that the moral virtues of prudence, justice, fortitude and temperance, are likewise communicated to us at the same moment. It is well to know from whence this teaching comes. It is equally important to understand that the moral virtues endow us with a supernatural proximate *power* of eliciting or drawing forth supernatural acts, and not, as some imagine, a *facility or ease* in drawing forth supernatural acts. In other words, the moral virtues are not given to make supernatural acts easier, but rather to make them possible. To acquire the facility of action which acquired habits give, one must perform repeated acts of such virtues.

It seems necessary here to state that there are such things as *natural virtues,* good habits acquired through the frequent repetition of acts which render easy the performance of morally good actions. There is an ocean of difference between the purely natural virtues and supernatural or infused virtues as they exist in the Christian soul and are communicated to the soul by the Holy Ghost's dwelling in us.

Elevated to the supernatural state, and having no other destiny than the Beatific Vision, we must tend thereto through acts performed under the influence of supernatural principles and of supernatural motives, thus, the virtues which the world knows as natural virtues must be practiced by us in a *supernatural* manner. As Father Garrigou-Lagrange says: "The Christian moral virtues are infused and, because of their formal object, are essentially distinct from the highest of acquired moral virtues described by the greatest philosophers ... There is an infinite difference between Aristotelian temperance, with *reason* as its only rule, and Christian temperance with the super-added rule of divine faith and supernatural prudence."[1]

With the foregoing well understood, it follows that we should note the number of such moral virtues.

There are four cardinal virtues and five principal virtues related to them. Let us look at them. They are:

(1) Prudence

(2) Justice $\left\{\begin{array}{l}\text{Religion} \\ \text{Obedience}\end{array}\right.$

(3) Fortitude

(4) Temperance $\left\{\begin{array}{l}\text{Meekness} \\ \text{Humility} \\ \text{Chastity}\end{array}\right.$

Since we are here, primarily, interested only in the infused moral virtue of *religion*, let us focus our attention upon it. At the outset, we notice that it is related to the virtue of *justice* which is defined as a moral supernatural virtue, which inclines the will to render unto others at all times what is strictly their due. From this definition it is plainly evident how *religion* is related to justice, especially if we note a definition of the virtue of religion: *"Religion*

---

(1)   Garrigou-Lagrange, Perfect. chret. & contemplation p. 62-75.

*is a moral, supernatural virtue that inclines the will to render to God the worship due Him by reason of His infinite excellence and of His sovereign dominion over us."*

The formal object of the virtue of religion is the acknowledgment of the infinite excellence of God, the perfect Being, on Whom all things depend and toward Whom all this must tend. Tanquerey in his excellent treatment of this topic distinguishes two acts in which religion inclines us toward God. The first he calls *interior,* and the second *exterior.* By *interior* acts of religion, we subject our soul with its faculties to God, chiefly our intellect and will. The acts naturally involve adoration, thanksgiving, penitence and petition. When these interior acts are expressed publicly, they are identified as *exterior* acts of religion.

The foremost of the exterior acts of religion is, without the shadow of a doubt, that of *sacrifice,* which is an exterior and social act, whereby the priest offers to God, in the name of the Church, an immolated victim in order to acknowledge His supreme dominion, to repair the offense offered to His Majesty, and to enter into communion with Him.

In the New Law there is but one sacrifice, that of the Mass, which, renewing the sacrifice of Calvary, offers to God an infinite homage and obtains for men all the graces they need. St. Bonaventure has beautifully expressed it in this way: "First of all God sends His Son down to us on the altar, then the Church sends Him up to the Father, to make intercession for sinners."

To this principal act are added the public prayers offered in the name of the Church by her representatives:

the Divine Office, Benediction of the Blessed Sacrament, private vocal prayers, etc.

Since God made man for His glory, all creatures are bound to give glory to God. For man it is an especial duty. Unfortunately, as we noted earlier, the majority of mankind, absorbed in business or pleasure, devotes but little time to the worship of God, so it was necessary to choose from among men certain special representatives acceptable to Almighty God, that they might, not only in their own name but in the name of society, render God the religious duties to which He has a right. *This is the glorious role of the priest!*

The priest is chosen by God from among his fellow-men to be a *mediator* and an *ambassador* between heaven and earth, charged with glorifying God, with offering Him the homages of all creatures and with drawing down upon the earth God's graces and blessings. These are his principal tasks, his duties of state, his profession, his duty of justice, as St. Paul explains: "For every high priest taken from among men is ordained for men in the things that appertain to God, that he may offer up gifts and sacrifices for sins." [1]

It is for this reason that the Church has confided to her priests two great means of exercising the virtue of religion, the Sacrifice of the Mass and the Divine Office.

The thought alone of being chosen by God, to act as His ambassador or intermediary between mankind and the Creator, Redeemer, and Sanctifier, should stir incalculable numbers of young men to ascertain for certain whether or

(1) Hebr. 5:1.

not they are so called to serve in this sublime capacity. Every other honor or dignity is paled thereby into insignificance. The very thought of this idea caused St. Cyril of Alexandria to cry out: "Divine are the offices confided to the priest," and St. Ignatius, Martyr, to say in his Epistle to the Christians of Smyrna that the priesthood is the most sublime of all created dignities, or to use his exact words: "The apex of dignities is the priesthood." According to Cassian, the priest is exalted above all earthly sovereignties, and above all celestial heights — he is inferior only to God.

The dignity of the priesthood is estimated from the exalted nature of his offices. You see, a priest is a minister destined by God to be a public ambassador of the whole Church, to honor God, and to obtain His graces for all the faithful. How is God accorded the highest honors, how does the priest chiefly obtain God's graces for all the faithful? By the Holy Sacrifice of the Mass.

Man, through his original sin, was lost. An offended God could have left him in his sad state and would have done him no injustice, but an all-merciful God chose rather to save man. The means were altogether unique. In His infinite Wisdom God issued a decree through which, by one act, He could save man, safeguard justice, and obtain perfect glorification from creation, which thereby would attain in full the end for which it had been placed in being. This decree was that the Son, the Second Person of the Blessed Trinity, should become a priest, that is, that the Son of God should assume human nature and be a representation of the whole human race, and in such a role, perform a priestly function through which God, on the one hand, would be glorified, praised and thanked to the highest possible degree, and that man, on the other hand, would pay his enormous debt and be redeemed.

That this decree was conceived and carried out by order of God, the Father, and with the cooperation of the Holy Ghost, is attested to by the second prayer that the priest says before Holy Communion, as noted in the Ordinary of the Mass, and which states: "according to the will of the Father, through the cooperation of the Holy Ghost."[1] Thus, through a decree through which Jesus Christ became Man, God draws from creation, through His official Priest, the greatest possible praise and glory.

One Person, alone, has been chosen by God to renew in its fullness, between His fellow-men and the Divine Majesty, the connection rent asunder by sin, and at the same time to render the Most Holy Trinity all Its due honor; and this incomparable Priest is Jesus Christ. Since man had sinned, Christ the Priest, Whose mission it was to advance God's glory, had to achieve His mission, which was to blot out sin and make reparation for its commission. For this reason the Wisdom of God decreed that the essential act of Christ's Priesthood should be a bloody sacrifice, the sacrifice of the Cross.

Since the priesthood's sole reason for being is the offering of sacrifice, Christ, the Son of God, was therefore a priest solely to offer a sacrifice to the Divinity in the name of mankind. That He is a priest was tenderly inscribed by St. Paul under inspiration of the Holy Ghost:

(1) "ex voluntate Patris, cooperante Spiritu Sancto."

"We have such a High Priest, Who is set on the right hand of the Throne of Majesty in the heavens, a Minister of the Holies" (Heb. 8:1); "He hath delivered Himself for us, an Oblation and a Sacrifice to God for an odour of sweetness" (Eph. 5:2). Jesus Christ, the Supreme Priest, offers but one sacrifice, the sacrifice of Calvary. On the cross He immolates Himself to His Father that sovereign dominion and infinite power of God may have absolute recognition. This abasement of the Man-God is, then, a recognition of the divine supremacy that is official, evident to the senses and effective, consisting in an act of *adoration* that is incalculable, an act of *petition* that is a sublime odour of sweetness, an act of *reparation* that is complete, and an act of *thanksgiving* that is infinite.

It is in the plan of God that Calvary's boons should be spread throughout the world in every age through the Mass, the daily renewal of the only great Sacrifice. Christ's Eucharistic Sacrifice gives to each one of us the chance and the right to take part in the redeeming sacrifice of Calvary, by permitting us to take a personal role in it, as truly as if we had been standing beneath the Cross on the first Good Friday. And this is where the priests in our human society come into the subject.

Our Lord is *the* Priest, the only Priest, of Himself absolute and unqualified that ever has existed and that ever shall exist, offering the only sacrifice ever exacted by God as solely satisfactory and sufficing, all other sacrifices, such as those of the Old Testament, having been accepted only as figures of the sacrifice of Calvary. Now, since Christ did not will to prolong throughout the ages His material earthly existence, visibly to perform His priestly ministry in human society, He has chosen certain men Whom he marks with an indelible character, by virtue of which He confers upon them the power of exercising, in a visible manner, His supernatural function amongst mankind.

Actually, our Lord and His priest form a moral unit, accomplishing one and the same act, to which Christ's power gives efficacy, the priest's presence, visibility. Since priests are the instruments used by the Sovereign Priest in His priestly activities among men, and since they are in direct contact with the source of all supernatural good, from which they draw the choicest graces, sublime is their dignity.

St. Alphonsus reminds us that the entire Church cannot give to God as much honor, nor obtain so many graces, as a single priest celebrating a single Mass; for the greatest honor that the whole Church without priests could give to God would consist in offering to Him in sacrifice the lives of all men. But, of what value are the lives of all mankind compared with the sacrifice of the Son of God, which is a sacrifice of infinite value? By the sacrifice of one Mass, a priest gives greater honor to God than all the angels and saints, along with the Blessed Virgin Mary, have given or shall give to Him, for their worship cannot be of infinite value like that which the priest celebrating Mass on the altar offers to God.

In a wondrous burst of enthusiasm, St. Alphonsus cries out that "Jesus has died to institute the priesthood. It was not necessary for the Redeemer to die in order to save the world; a drop of His Blood, a single tear, or prayer, was sufficient to procure salvation for all; for such a prayer, being of infinite worth should be sufficient to save not one but a thousand worlds. But to institute the priesthood, the death of Jesus Christ has been necessary. Had He not died, where should we find the Victim that the priests of the New Law now offer? A Victim altogether holy and immaculate, capable of giving to God an honor worthy of God?" What a powerfully moving thought!

If more young men dwelt upon the dignity of the priesthood, more would answer God's call. The dignity and grandeur of this vocation beggars description. The priesthood transcends in dignity, as St. Bernard notes, "all the dignities of kings, of emperors and of angels." It transcends in grandeur and power all other created dignities. The *grandeur* is estimated from the consideration that impelled St. Ignatius, Martyr, to say: "Priests are the dispensers of divine graces and the associates of God," and the *power* is high-lighted by these words of St. Lawrence Justinian, who, speaking of priests, says: "O how very great is their power. A word falls from their lips and the Body of Christ is there substantially formed from the matter of bread, and the Incarnate Word descended from heaven is found really present on the table of the altar! Never did divine goodness give such power to angels. The angels abide by order of God, but the priests take Him in their hands, distribute Him to the faithful, and partake of Him as food for themselves." The thought that poured in upon the fertile mind of St. Augustine in this regard is found in these words he wrote: "O wonderful dignity of the priests, in their hands, as in the womb of the Blessed Virgin, the Son of God becomes incarnate;" and it was with a sort of whispered timidity that St. Bernardine of Siena wrote: "Holy Virgin, excuse me, for I speak not against thee: the Lord raised the priesthood above thee."

When Christ ascended into heaven, He left His priests after Him to hold on this earth His place of mediator between God and mankind, particularly on the altar. St. Augustine expresses himself in these words regarding priests: "You hold the place of Christ; you are therefore His lieutenants." St. Augustine's choice of the word "lieutenant" is brilliant. It is made up of two words from the French — *lieu* - place, and *tenant* - holding — thus a lieutenant is one who supplies the place of a superior. In confirmation of this interpretation of the role of priests, we note that in the Council of Milan, St. Charles Borromeo called priests "the representatives of the person of God on earth."

When the angel appeared to St. Joseph to reveal to him the mystery of the incarnation of our Lord and Mary's role in it, he said: "And she shall bring forth a Son; and thou shalt call His name Jesus. For He shall save His people from their sins." (Matth. 1:21).

As the Eternal Father, sent Jesus, His only begotten Son, to save people from their sins, so in like manner this great mission which Jesus Christ has received from His Eternal Father He has communicated to His priests. "Jesus," says Tertullian, "invests the priests with His own powers." Thus, the priest holds the place of the Lord Himself, when by saying, *"Ego te absolvo"* — "I absolve thee," he absolves from sin. The very thought of this impelled St. Augustine to say, "To sanctify a sinner is a greater work than to create heaven and earth." According to St. Augustine's great benefactor, St. Ambrose, a priest in giving absolution performs the very office of the Holy Ghost in the sanctification of souls. When our Lord was about to give His Apostles the power of absolving, the Risen Redeemer "breathed on them and said to them, 'Receive ye the Holy Ghost: whose sins you shall forgive, they are forgiven them; and whose sins you shall retain, they are retained.' " (John 20:22). Here again is further proof that when Christ gave to His priests His own Spirit, that is, the Holy Ghost, the Sanctifier of souls, He made them *His* own coadjutors or ambassadors.

How can anyone read the foregoing without being moved to surrender himself to serve God in His priesthood if he be called by God to play such a role? To be called to the priesthood is a dignity beyond all dignities. God wills that all men should be saved, but not in the same manner. As in heaven He has distinguished different degrees of glory, so on earth He has established different states of life, as so many different ways of gaining heaven. On account of the great ends for which it has been instituted, namely, to watch over the honor of His divine Majesty and to procure the salvation of souls, the priesthood is of all these the most noble, the most exalted and sublime.

If the question that comes to your mind now is: "How does one know if he has a vocation to the priesthood?" then the following chapters will be most helpful.

## CHAPTER FOUR

## ... BUT I HAVE CHOSEN YOU!

It is uncertain, in the silence of the Bible, whether sacrifice was at first commanded by God Himself of our sin-stained First Parents and their children, or grew out of human consciousness of guilt and the innate feeling of need of atonement. The first recorded sacrifice is mentioned in Genesis, Chapter IV, verse 4, where we read of the sacrifices offered by Adam's sons, Cain and Abel. The next time sacrifice is mentioned is when Noah came out of the ark: "And Noah built an altar unto the Lord: and taking of all cattle and fowls that were clean, offered holocausts upon the altar. And the Lord smelled a sweet savour, and said: 'I will no more curse the earth for the sake of man: for the imagination and thought of man's heart are prone to evil from his youth: therefore I will no more destroy every living soul as I have done.'" (Gen. 8:20-21).

The first reference to God's having *commanded* the offering of a sacrifice was when He directed Abraham to prepare a cow, goat, ram, turtle-dove and pigeon, and a fire was sent from heaven to consume them. (Gen. 15:9).

Since sacrifices were to make up the principal ceremonies of the Old Testament, God chose one of the Twelve Tribes, the tribe of Levi, to be His priests. The tribe of Levi originally was composed of the three principal families, namely, the descendants of Gerson, Caath and Merari, Levi's three sons. Out of these the Lord chose the family of Caath, and out of this line, the house of Aaron, upon which He conferred the honor of the priesthood in perpetuity. The rest of the tribe was to wait on the priests, and to be employed in the minor duties of the tabernacle; so that while all the priests were Levites, not all the Levites were priests. What must be noted from the foregoing is that God had made a definite choice of a definite part of a tribe to serve Him as priests. The same is true of the kings of Israel, the patriarchs and prophets. Perhaps one of the most outstanding examples of God's choice of a definite man for a special task is to be found in the story of Jonas, one of the Old Testament prophets.

Ninive was one of the mightiest cities of ancient times. In it were temples, palaces, and houses for a great multitude of people; and beautiful gardens, and green fields where cattle were fed. Around the city were walls a hundred feet high. These walls so thick on the top that three chariots drawn by horses might be driven side by side. And towers were built above the walls, all around the city. There were fifteen hundred towers, each one being over two hundred feet high. On the top of the walls and in the towers, the Assyrian soldiers stood, to shoot arrows and darts at their enemies when they came to attack Ninive. But Ninive was a very wicked city.

One day God spoke to the prophet Jonas, saying, "Arise and go to Ninive the great city and preach in it: for the wickedness thereof is come up before Me." (Jonas 1:2). But Jonas did not want to go, and he fled to Joppe, a city by the sea. There he found a ship that was going to a far away country, and Jonas paid his fare and went into it, that he might flee to some place where he would not hear God speaking to him.

But when he sailed out on the sea, the Lord sent a great wind, and as a result a great storm, so that the ship was in danger of being broken into pieces. Then the sailors were afraid, and they prayed, each one to his idol, for help. They threw out, also, some of the ship's most valuable cargo to lighten it and keep it from sinking. While this was going on, Jonas was asleep in the lower part of the ship. In a short time, the captain came to him and awakened him, saying, "Why art thou fast asleep? Rise up, call upon thy God, if so be that God will think of us, that we may not perish."

Then the sailors began talking among themselves saying that there must be a wicked man aboard and that such a one, if he could be found, should be cast overboard. Well, they drew lots and the lot fell upon Jonas, and they began immediately to question him: "Tell us for what cause this evil is upon us? What is thy business? Of what country art thou and whither goest thou? Of what people art thou?" And Jonas replied: "I am a Hebrew, and I fear the Lord the God of heaven, Who made both the sea and the dry land." Then the prophet told the sailors to cast him overboard because he knew that he was the cause of their danger and distress. The sailors tried to row to the shore to let Jonas off near the land, but the storm was so fierce that they could not make any headway. Finally, they cast Jonas overboard, and a large fish God had prepared swallowed Jonas up, and there he remained for three days. From the depths of the insides of that monster, Jonas prayed, confessed his sins, and God heard him and commanded the creature of the sea to cast him out on the dry land. Then the Lord spoke to the prophet a second time saying: "Arise, and go to Ninive the great city: and preach in it the preaching that I bid thee." (Jonas 3:2).

This time Jonas set about to do as God had asked of him, and the whole city of Ninive, made up of more than one hundred and twenty thousand souls, from the King to the lowliest peasant prayed, put on sack-cloth and ashes and did penance and were spared total destruction because they believed the threatening words of the prophet.

One thing stands in bold relief in the story of Jonas the prophet, and it is that God often sees in one person qualities He can use to carry out His plans for mankind, and He pursues that person with surprising force. Certainly, on the face of it, Jonas could not be considered a strong character. He was selfish, timid, self-conscious, fearful that he might be laughed at for trying to get a whole sinful city to do penance, or that he might be called a false prophet. The moral is, that God can use anyone He wishes to do His work. Alone, the individual may be totally inadequate, but working as God's instrument in the work of saving souls, miracles take place.

Far too many, I fear, looking at themselves and being conscious of their short-comings, refuse God's invitation to be His disciples. Moses was a most unlikely person to perform the task God decided to confide to him. He was a man most hunted by the Egyptians, since he had slain the Egyptian he had seen mistreating a Hebrew, yet God chose him to face the Pharao and to ask him to let the Hebrew people depart from Egypt. Moses tried his best to dodge the task. He said that the Jewish people would not accept him as their leader and spokesman: "They will not believe me, nor hear my voice. But they will say: 'The Lord hath not appeared to thee.'" (Exod. 4:1,2). It was then that God showed that when He confides a task to a person He supplies at the same time all the necessary means to carry it out, and at times the power to confirm his mission with miracles. In Moses' case He told him to throw the rod which he was carrying in his hand to the ground. When he did, the rod turned into a serpent. Then God told Moses to pick up the serpent by the tail, and while with some misgivings Moses did as he was bidden the serpent turned back again into a rod.

Moses tried one more thing. He pleaded his incapacity of speaking well: "I beseech Thee, Lord, I am not eloquent from yesterday and the day before: and since thou hast spoken to thy servant, I have more impediment and slowness of tongue." The Lord said to him: "Who made man's mouth? Or who made the dumb and the deaf, the seeing and the blind? Did not I? Go therefore, and I will be in thy mouth: and I will teach thee what thou shaʼt speak." (Gen. 4:10,12).

When God chose Jeremias, the Old Testament priest, to be a prophet, He plainly stated that He had foreordained him for special work: "Before I formed thee in the bowels of thy mother, I knew thee: and before thou camest forth out of the womb, I sanctified thee and made thee a prophet unto the nations." (Jer. 1:5).

As Moses too had tried to side-step the responsibilities God had chosen to confide to him, so in like manner, Jeremias tried to avoid serving God in the capacity of a prophet, saying, "Ah, ah, ah, Lord God, behold, I cannot speak for I am a child." And the Lord said to Jeremias: "Say not 'I am a child': for thou shalt go to all that I shall send thee, and whatsoever I shall command thee, thou shalt speak. Be not afraid of their presence; for I am with thee to deliver thee," saith the Lord. "And the Lord put forth His hand and touched my mouth. And the Lord said to me: 'Behold I have given My words in thy mouth.'" (Jer. 1:6-9).

Two things are clear from the story of the call of Jeremias to be one of God's prophets: (1) that it is God Himself Who chooses those whom He desires to do His work, and (2) when He chooses a person to perform a task He provides the means for and help in its accomplishment. Nothing illustrates the second consideration more clearly than the story of Aser, the eighth son of Jacob. You see, when Moses was dividing the land among the Twelve Tribes, when he came to Aser he added, "Thy shoes shall be of iron and brass." (Deut. 55:25). A little geographical research will help make the meaning of the warning plain.

The territory allotted to the tribe of Aser was hilly and rugged. Common sandals made of wood or leather would never endure the wear and tear of the sharp flinty rocks. The terrain assigned to the tribe of Aser demanded some special kind of shoes, hence the warning: "Thy shoes shall be of iron and brass." When God assigns certain duties and responsibilities He supplies all the necessary means of fulfilling them. If Aser's territory was rugged, so rugged that shoes of brass and iron would be necessary, then God would have to provide these materials. And, indeed He did. Providentially, the territory assigned to the tribe of Aser abounded in metals.

It might be in order here to define what is meant by "vocation," in general, and a vocation to the priesthood, in particular.

A vocation, in general, might be defined as *a call from God to that state of life which He has destined for each soul.* Thus, it is evident that each soul has his vocation predetermined in the mind of God. It must be held as certain, says St. Thomas, "All things are subject to Divine Providence; not only in general, in broad lines, but rather in every detail." How could God, Who foresees the death of a bird and Who permits not a hair of one's head to fall without His permission, abandon to mere caprice and chance human beings made in His image and likeness? On the contrary, He has fixed a place for each person to occupy in this world. When Joan of Arc was about to leave Vaucouleurs she said to the crowd: "Do not weep; it was for this that I was born." All of us were born to accomplish some special task, a task that no one can do for us, or as St. Paul puts it: "But everyone hath his proper gift from God: one after this manner, and another after that." (1 Cor. 7:7).

It is a stirring truth that every man has a distinct vocation, a personal vocation, which may seem to resemble that of others, but which in reality is not precisely the same.

That there is a hierarchy in the matter of vocations is proven from the infallible teachings of the Church: "If anyone says that the marriage state should be preferred to the state of virginity or the state of celibacy, and that it is better to live in the married state than in virginity or celibacy, let him be anathema." (Council of Trent), but this does not say one cannot find perfection in marriage, as well as in the priesthood; the chances, however, are better in the priesthood. St. Paul bears this out when he writes: "He that is without a wife is solicitous for the things that belong to the Lord, how he may please God. But he that is with a wife is solicitous for the things of the world, how he may please his wife, and he is divided." (1 Cor. 7:33-34).

But that some are called to the priesthood, the religious life, celibacy, or the state of virginity, while others are called to the married state, is nicely proven by this marvelous story. It seems that in 1858, two devout young men, Alphonsus Fellion and Felix Christopher, left Bellmont, (Loire) in France, on a pilgrimage to the parish where the saintly Curé of Ars was pastor.

The young men spent the entire day in prayer in the church of Ars, but they could not get to confession to the saintly Curé due to the enormous crowd. They decided late in the evening to return to their hotel room and planned to go to the church early in the morning. As they knelt to say their night prayers, Felix was surprised to hear voices singing the *Gloria in Excelsis* apparently coming from the church which was nearby. Noticing the dismay of his companion, Alphonsus said, "What's the matter?"

"Do you not hear the singing coming from the church?" asked Felix.

"Ah, you're dreaming, said Alphonsus. Then, thinking he might hear the voices, he opened the window. He was disappointed upon hearing nothing, but the heavenly voices were even clearer to Felix. "If I do not hear the voices as you hear them, it may be because I didn't get to confession. Perhaps I am not in the state of grace," said Alphonsus sadly.

At one A. M. when the Curé of Ars began to hear confessions, the young men were there. As Felix knelt before the humble Curé the saint began with these words: "Oh my child, you were very happy last night and your companion was sad . . . you will not marry or be a priest or religious by vocation, yet you will do much good in the world. It is for that reason that the good God gave you the marked preference. Your companion is destined to marry, but, nevertheless, he too is very pleasing to God. Do you know why the angels were singing last night? At that moment a great sinner was converted."

When Alphonsus presented himself to the Curé of Ars, the saint said to him: "My child, you were sad last night when you could not hear the chant of the angels. Nevertheless, the good God loves you very much."

"Father, I wish to be a religious Brother," said Alphonsus, to which the Curé replied: "No, my child. You are destined to a life in marriage. When you return home to your parish, the first young lady who speaks to you will be your wife. You will be a good Christian husband."[1]

As the Cure' of Ars directed, Alphonsus Fillion married on January 13, 1863, and remained an admirable Christian until his death on January 29, 1884.

Felix Christopher lived a saintly celibate life as a layman and was an edification to all who knew him. He died on April 3, 1913, at the age of seventy.[2]

This story gives evidence of two things: (1) the remarkable gift given by God to the Curé of Ars of knowing heaven'y secrets, and (2) that there is a state of life to which God has destined each soul.

Since there is a special state of life destined for each human being by the Creator, if we would be happy and make a success of life, we must seek out God's will in our regard and willingly do what God wants us to do. It would be nigh unto blasphemy to say that God destines man for a certain state and then leaves him without any way of knowing exactly which state he is to embrace. This *direct* call such as that given the Apostles, or the *miraculous* call of a Paul, or the inspired direction given by the Curé of Ars to the two young men mentioned above, are rarities, indeed. Ordinarily, *vocation occurs when, under the influence of grace, with docility and freedom, the soul makes*

(1)  Canon Francis Trochu, Les Intuitions du Cure d'Ars 3e serie, pp. 9-12

(2)  Ibid.

*the decision chosen for it by God, and this through criteria
which are objective, external and valid, though not of themselves conclusive.*

It is imperative that one pray to know his true vocation. Let God know you desire more than anything else to
do His Will. Tell Him you are ready and willing, despite
every obstacle, to do anything and everything that He may
ask of you in connection with your future. In turn, for such
an offer, God in His Goodness will give you every help you
need to make your life purposeful, successful, and peaceful.
So the key word here is *prayer.*

It is mysterious the way God makes His will known.
St. Alphonsus says: "Care little from whence the move-
ment comes: because God has many ways to call one into
His service. Some are moved by sermons, others from reading good books. Some have been called to say 'yes' through
the sacred words of the Gospel, as were St. Francis and
St. Anthony; others are called through illness or misfortune."
Reverend Jerome Planus, S.J., recounts how a lordly young
gentleman, mounted on a splendid horse, was strutting
before some young ladies with the idea of impressing them.
His horse bolted and the rider was thrown in the mud.
Extremely confused and humiliated, the young man right
there and then resolved to enter a religious order, which
he did, by the way, and lived a saintly life.

There is another point we must consider. Remember
that it was *God Himself* who called Moses, Jonas, and Jeremias to serve Him, and that these men were convinced that
they would be failures, until, in each case, God told them
He would be with them to strengthen them. One shudders

to think of what might have happened if Moses had refused to lead the Chosen People out of Egypt into the Promised Land. Ninive with its hundred and twenty thousand people might well have been destroyed from the face of the earth as were Sodom and Gomorrah had not Jonas after his great lesson, returned and preached penance to them. Wouldn't it be a frightful burden for one's conscience if God's call to the priesthood went unheeded by anyone today? Archbishop Neil McNeil of Toronto, Canada, used to say that the average priest by his prayers and works saves four thousand souls, and if this be so, what a burden for someone to carry who refuses Christ's invitation to follow Him!

In my first years in the priesthood, I was stationed as a pastor on the Canadian prairies. One day when I was out on visitation I was driving along in my little old Ford coupé and I saw I was coming to a fork in the road. One road went to the left, the other to the right. Just before I came to the fork in the road I saw a man standing with a knapsack on his back. Now, keep the picture well in mind. The man was about one hundred yards from the fork. Had I been five minutes later, he would have taken the right road and I the left. In any case, there he stood. I stopped the car as one always did in the West. There was something about the West that made you trust everyone. No one in my day even locked a door. It would be nothing to come home after a trip to the city and find that someone had s'ept in your bed and had left a note thanking you for the hospitality. I never lost a penny or even a stamp.

Well, back to the story. I heard the back of the car open after I stopped, and the man dropped his knapsack in and closed the lid, and slid in beside me on the seat. When he got a look at the collar he said: "Have I fallen into the hands of the clergy again?" His second statement start'ed me a little: "Will there ever be enough work for peop'.e or must we go on just being numbers?" I began to think I had picked up a twenty-two carat nut. I said nothing and just kept driving. After a spell that seemed like an eternity, the man began to recite in perfect Latin the prayers the priest says at the foot of the altar at Holy Mass. He continued with the *Magnificat* and *Benedictus.* Turning to him I said, "Are you a priest?"

"No," he replied.

"A brother?" I queried.

"No," came the answer.

"Well, just who are you, and where did you learn all those Latin prayers?" I asked.

Then began an intriguing story. He had been born in India of British parents. Both parents having died, an aunt, who was a religious, had him brought to England. He was sent to the great Stoneyhurst University and upon graduation he decided to go to Canada. First he lost all his money and then his faith, and so he drifted in search of work from pillar to post.

I brought him home to the little rectory, cooked him supper (don't laugh — out West, in my day, you cooked your own meals), induced him to get straight with God and to make his Easter duty, which he did, and I may say that I have never seen a person receive Holy Communion with more faith and devotion than he did the next morning. Then, with the few dollars I could spare, I drove him down to the railway station to catch a freight train East (some of my parishioners worked for the railway and they conveniently didn't see him enter an empty open box-car), but just before he got on that train, he turned and said, "Father, you'll never know what meeting you has meant to me. Do you remember that clump of bushes near the fork in the road where I met you? (I did remember, for any size bush in those days on the flat prairie land stood out like the Washington Monument). "Well," he said, "I had finally decided to end it all," and as he spoke, he drew from his top jacket pocket, a long straight razor. "But now" the man said, "the world looks different."

You know, I've often wondered what would have happened had I not been passing *that* spot on the road where he stood; what would have happened had I passed him by; what responsibility I might have had for that soul had I refused the call to the priesthood? I leave the answers to you.

But, getting back to Moses, Jonas, and Jeremias, their vocations were miraculous. So was St. Paul's. You recall how, one day while he was in search of new victims, he was enveloped in a blinding light, and how, as he fell to the ground, he heard a voice saying to him: "Saul, Saul, why persecutest thou Me?" and realizing that there was something divine about this voice, he answered, "Who art Thou, Lord?" and the voice came back, "I am Jesus Whom thou persecutest." And trembling and astonished Saul said: "Lord, what wilt Thou have me to do?" And the Lord said to him: "Arise and go into the city, and there you shall be told what thou must do." (Acts 9:3-7)

Rising to his feet, he realized he was blind, and so the once proud Saul was led into the city of Damascus by his companions who had heard the voice from heaven, but who had seen no one.

The strange part of the conversion of St. Paul lies in the fact that in spite of his question to our Lord — "Lord, what wilt Thou have me to do?", our Lord just sent him into the city saying that someone *there* would tell him what to do.

Why didn't our Lord, Himself, tell him? It would have saved a lot of trouble. You see, our Lord had to appear to Ananias, a disciple of the Lord, and tell him in a vision that He was going to send Saul to him for instruction. And see, the people all knew Saul as a persecutor of the faithful, and Ananias would rather have encountered anyone but Saul. In any case, our Lord dispelled his fears by saying: "Go thy way: for this man is to me a vessel of election, to carry My Name before the Gentiles and Kings and the children of Israel. For I will show him how much he must suffer for My Name's sake" (Acts 9:15-16).

Here again are two powerful lessons: (1) God does not always choose the most likely candidates for the priesthood from our standards or points of view. In every one He does call, however, He sees something that He can use to promote the glory of His Father and the salvation of souls; (2) that He wants us to learn that, as Pope Leo XIII says: "God in His infinite Providence has decreed that men for the most part should be saved by men; hence He has appointed that those whom He calls to a loftier degree of holiness should be led thereto by men, in order that, as

St. John Chrysostom says, 'we should be taught by God through men.'" The moral of this second lesson is that we ought not decide such an important thing as to whether or not we are called to the priesthood all by ourselves, but rather we should consult with our confessor or spiritual director for guidance in this matter. He who is his own lawyer has a fool for a client! Be honest, now, your judgment is not always the best in other things so how can you be sure you are right in saying you do not have a vocation to the priesthood? You had better be sure. Many souls may be dependent upon you.

But I can hear you say, "Father, if I was knocked out of my Jaguar, blinded, and told that I had a vocation to the priesthood by Christ Himself, I'd have no trouble making up my mind either." Well, to tell you the truth, the miraculous call to the priesthood or religious life *is* rare, indeed, but God can use other means to enlighten our minds. Take for instance the case of St. Ignatius of Loyola.

Ignatius was born at Loyola, in Northern Spain, in 1491, the eighth son in a family of thirteen children. Educated at the court of Ferdinand, and in the train of the Duke of Najara, Ignatius was deeply imbued with the spirit of his nation and class. He aspired to knightly renown, the glitter of arms, and the fame of heroism.

The profession of arms seemed to open to him a field in which every desire of his heart, the noblest impulses of his nature would find their legitimate scope. Generous, just, and honorable, he was beloved by the soldiers he commanded. In the Providence of God, Ignatius at the age of twenty-nine was wounded in both legs, at the defense of

Pampeluna in 1521. During his long confinement he read the glowing stories of love and heroism, interspersed with the graver study of the life of Christ and some of the Saints, in Spanish, the only language with which he was then acquainted. The deeds of St. Francis and St. Dominic caught his fancy. They came as a revelation to him and he began to feel called to establish an army to do battle on earth under the command of Christ's Vicar in the sacred cause of the God of hosts. Some writers say that it was when he had read and pondered over the words he found in one of his spiritual books quoting the Bible — "What doth it profit a man if he gain the whole world and suffer the loss of his soul?" (Matth. 16:26) that he decided to quit the world and work only for God's glory. Be this as it may, we do know that Ignatius went to the Benedictine Abbey at Montserrat and laid his sword at the feet of our Lady's statue. The rest of the story of the founding of the incomparable Society of Jesus is history.

The call Ignatius received to serve God in the priesthood was brought about in a different manner than the call of St. Paul, but the end result was the same.

The twelve Apostles were *directly* called to the priesthood by our Lord Himself during His public life on this earth. St. Paul's call was miraculously manifested by our Lord *after* He had ascended into heaven. There are other instances of this sort of call in the annals of the Church, such as evidenced in the case of St. Norbert.

St. Ignatius of Loyo'a, on the other hand, received his ca'l to the priesthood in an *indirect* manner. It was during his convalescence that God spoke to him through a few striking lines he read in a book. Stirred as he had never been before, his will, assisted by divine grace, was moved to resolve to quit the world to serve as a soldier of Christ in His priesthood. This second type of call is much more common than the miraculous call. Many there are who came to a realization of having a true vocation to the priesthood only after a serious illness, a disaster of some sort or other to the individual or his fami.y, or some other stirring experience that caused them to see the true value of things in the light of eternity. Many G.I.'s, for instance, sickened by what modern warfare entailed, were moved to enter seminaries and novitiates after our last two major wars. Others, like the soldiers who served in the Korea "Police action", seeing first-hand the need for priests in the foreign lands they had visited, returned to civilian life determined to surrender themselves to serve as priests and missionaries in all stations of the world. God, you see, made His call felt by letting such young men see the great need for more priests and by letting them see the benefits conferred upon the natives through the ministry of the missionaries.

Thus far we have considered several of the means God uses to direct a man into that vocation He has willed for him, but there is still another and by far the most common means. This third way could be loosely described as a divine invitatory motion manifesting God's will of good pleasure to a man by the light of reason en'ightened by the grace of faith, and moving the will to embrace the ecclesiastical state. The ways in which God extends His invitation; the peculiarity of time and place, or age, and of providential

circumstances are infinite. The very wording of the foregoing statement indicates that God does not force, but
rather draws by the cords of love, and that He breathes
where He will, and thus, such a vocation is a mystery of
God's infinite love, a mystery of predilection.

Perhaps one of the greatest evils that has ever struck
us is the all-too-common belief that no one has a vocation
to the religious or ecclesiastical life unless he has a "sensible
attraction." Equally damaging is the oft-related phrase
that you have a vocation if you hear an "inner voice" calling
you. The net result of this "inner voice" idea is that you
have young people sitting around waiting to hear "inner
voices" and you know that if anyone did hear voices, he'd
be off like a shot to the nearest psychiatrist. Only last
summer, after I had said Mass in a little country parish
church, I turned to the tiny altar boy and said: "I suppose
you are going to be a priest when you grow up." And
with all the definitiveness of a Philadelphia lawyer, he said:
"Well, I ain't heard no voice yet!" Where did he get that
idea of "a voice"? — from the many little leaflets, adver-
tisements and "comic" type propaganda productions that
include such statements as: "If You Hear the Voice, Answer
It" — "If You Hear the Call, Answer It," etc.

Thanks to the great and saintly Pius X, the *"sensible
attraction"* and *"inward fascination"* theories were exploded.
Under his direction the controversy revolving around these
theories was settled by a special commission of Cardinals.
The matter came to a head over a published work entitled
*La Vocation Sacerdotal,* written by Canon Joseph Lahitton.
At the time the book was written (and even today) spiritual

writers had been accustomed to insist that the necessity of a strong interior attraction for the priestly state was a certain sign of the Divine Call, and maintained if this sensible urging of the Holy Ghost, this desire and longing to be a priest of The Most High were wanting, there could not be any real vocation, and delusion was to be feared. All sorts of emphasis were laid on the fact that since a vocation was a free gift of God, an act by which He selects some in preference to others, this choice must be made known interiorly to the soul so favored; without this interior vocation it would be presumption and the height of folly to aspire to such a dignity.

Now, in 1909, Canon Lahitton wrote in his book that a vocation to the priesthood did not consist in any subjective feeling or inclination ("attrait"-attraction) for that state, but was manifested by a certain fitness or suitability in the candidate and that it was the ministers of the Church who really gave the vocation in the calling to Holy Orders. He held that nothing further was required in the aspirant for a legitimate call from the Bishop than the three conditions laid down by St. Thomas and St. Alphonsus — namely, probity of life, sufficient knowledge, and the right intention. Well, naturally, this was such a departure from the common teaching that the matter was taken to Rome.

St. Pius X, as we said, appointed a special commission of Cardinals to examine the question and the finding was in favor of Canon Lahitton, and the judgment was formally sanctioned by the decree of July 2, 1912. From this decree of the Holy See it is now certain:

1. That a vocation to the priesthood *does not necessarily* include any interior inclination of the person or prompting of the Holy Ghost.

2. That all that is required from aspirants to ordination is a right intention, and such fitness of nature and grace as evidenced in integrity of life, and a sufficient learning as well as a well-founded hope of his rightly discharging the obligation of the priesthood.

3. That, given these conditions, a true vocation is unquestionably conferred by the Bishop at the moment of Ordination.

Canon Lahitton's whole purpose in bringing up this question at all was to combat one particular theory on vocation which had long been prevalent and is preva'ent today to the detriment of the Church, and that is the "attraction theory." Its advocates, as we said above, maintained that a vocation to the priesthood consists essentially in a mysterious attraction by the Holy Ghost — an attraction which is felt in the depths of the soul and which makes the recipient profoundly certain that God is calling him. Unless one is conscious of such a quasi-mystical attraction, they maintain, he may not even think of aspiring to the clerical state, while on the other hand, he who does have it or feel it may demand that the gates of the sanctuary swing wide open to him; that he has a right to ordination and that the Church must accept this divinely infused attraction as final and decisive. It was against this theory that Canon Lahitton fought and won. In the decree of Ju'y 2, 1912, a death blow was delivered to the attraction theory.

But let us take care not to read into the decree more than is in it. It does not say that there need be *no* invitations of the Holy Spirit, nor does it imply that an interior divine vocation in any sense is excluded by the fact that only a right intention and fitness are required of candidates to the priesthood. To make the decree mean the first thing would be the same as to say that there is no need of divine grace to prepare a candidate worthily for the priesthood, while to make the decree imply the second idea would be the same as saying a person could aspire to the priesthood with a right supernatural intention and cultivate the virtues which form the ecclesiastical spirit without special graces given by God for this express and precise purpose.

Regarding the vocation God wishes men to follow, He manifests His will, as we have already noted, in many different ways. In the case of St. Paul, the manifestation was miraculously extraordinary, but such a manifestation of God's will is extraordinary, and therefore a way which we have no right to claim. St. Ignatius of Loyola, on the other hand, experienced a sudden illumination of the mind given by God in His grace, so that he seemed as it were, to be moved to the service of God without need for any protracted reasoning about the matter. God knew the type of person He was dealing with in Ignatius of Loyola, but this procedure would not be without possibility of delusion in the cases of others and, in the absence of genuine grace, it could conceivably arise from a strong emotional experience such as during a mission or a retreat. The normal way, which is the ordinary procedure in God's providence relative to a vocation in life, is more safe and sure.

The normal thing for a man to do in determining a vocation to the priesthood is to think out the matter in the calm time of prayer in the presence of God. He must ask himself if he is convinced that God has given him the grace of a vocation to the priesthood. When he poses that question to himself he must consider whether he has the right intention — such as the greater glory of God, His service, the salvation of souls, and the salvation of his own soul; in other words, does he feel he is doing something pleasing to God? Is he spiritually, physically, mentally and emotionally equipped for such a life? Has he the education necessary, or at least has he the capacity to be educated? Finally, has he good morals, integrity of life, and good character; and is he free from canonical impediments such as: illegitimacy, insanity, infamy, bigamy or is he a judge who has pronounced the death sentence, etc.? Generally speaking, then, nothing beyond the qualities implied in the above questions is required for a true vocation.

Suppose, now, that a young man answers affirmatively all the above questions, does that conclude the matter? No. He must ask himself whether it is God's will that he should be a diocesan priest or enter a religious community. Just as he thought out the question of the priesthood in general, in the calm time of prayer in the presence of God, so now, he must do likewise to determine how he will serve God in the priesthood. A prerequisite for his great decision must be the elimination of all human and natural motives that might endeavor to draw or to repel him from either the diocesan or the religious priesthood. As for the determining of his vocation to the priesthood in general, humble

prayer to God for the light to make the proper decision
and the strength to carry out that decision, so now in this
matter of the diocesan versus the religious priesthood,
prayer for the graces of God is most essential. God's grace
will not be lacking.

Let us be sure we know the difference between a
diocesan priest and a religious. Diocesan priests, sometimes
called "secular priests", live under the authority of a Bishop,
who in turn is charged by the Pope to administer a certain
determined territory called a diocese. It is the mission of
the diocesan clergy to collaborate with the Bishop in maintaining and spreading the faith among the inhabitants of
their district. Priests receive their Orders from the Bishop,
and so they are his spiritual sons. Diocesan priests con-
secrate themselves to the formation and teaching of youth,
as professors in universities, colleges, schools and seminaries;
they exercise the offices of chaplains in hospitals, religious
institutions, sanatoriums, jails and prisons; they are sometimes editors of papers and magazines, and chaplains to
the armed forces in peace and war, while the majority of
them confine their activities to preaching, administering
the Sacraments, and works of charity in the confines of
their particular parishes. Let us sum up as follows:

"The Pope," says St. Bernard, "is the high priest, the
prince among Bishops," and as such has jurisdiction over
the whole Church. The Bishops are the successors of the
Apostles with the task of guiding that portion of the Church
assigned to them by the Pope, and they assist the Pontiff
in the government of the universal Church. Diocesan priests
are the assistants of the Bishops, and they are divided into

(1) parish priests who have the care of souls in a particular district confided to them by a Bishop; (2) assistant pastors or curates, as they are often called, who, in turn, work under the direction of the pastor.

It should be stated here that a great many religious priests are called upon to collaborate with the Bishops in maintaining and spreading the faith. Religious priests exercising the active ministry under the direction of the Bishops must permit episcopal visitations, must have their appointment as pastors approved by the Bishop, and they are dependent on the Bishop for their faculties and jurisdiction. It is to the glory of the Church that there is such a close and amicable relationship between the diocesan and religious priests.

Before going into the matter of the difference between diocesan and religious priests, let us keep these two things well in mind: (1) the *Catholic priesthood* is exactly the same in and for a religious as it is in and for a member of the diocesan clergy, for both groups are called upon and privi'eged to perform the same central and essential Eucharistic work; (2) in the actually existing order of divine providence, the continuance of Christ's sacerdotal mission here on earth demands the activity of both groups. With these principles stated, let us turn our attention to the differences between the religious and the diocesan priesthood.

In Chapter Two we related the Scriptural story of the rich young man who inquired of our Lord what he had to do to get to heaven, and our Lord told him to keep the Commandments. When he told the Master he had done this from his earliest years, our Lord said: "If thou wilt be perfect, go, sell what thou hast and give to the poor, and come follow Me." (atth. 19:21). Those words laid the foundation for the religious life. First, notice that there is a *common* and a *perfect* way to love and serve God. The *common way* involves the faithful observance of the Commandments, while the *perfect way* involves the observance of the Commandments, plus the practice of the evangelical counsels through poverty, chastity and obedience. Secondly, recall that as we noted earlier, our Lord counselled — *"if thou wilt"*, He did not command.

It is from these inspired words that we come to a definition of the *religious state*. The religious state is defined in Canon 487 as "a permanent manner of community life by which the faithful undertake to observe not only the precepts common to all, but *also* the evangelical counsels by means of the vows of obedience, chastity and poverty." Now, if a person is to become perfect, his efforts to be good must be more than just spasmodic, occasional efforts; rather, they must be constant and continuous. Thus the degree of perfection one reaches must depend upon one's degree of stability in the love of God. Since the definition of the religious state uses the word *permanent,* which implies stability, it follows that this stability must be secured by *means of vows.*

The elements, therefore, of the religious state are:

(1) Stability of purpose by means of vows;

(2) The practice of the three evangelical counsels;

(3) Membership in a community.

Keep these thoughts in mind as you think over this

matter: (1) the religious state is a state that *leads* to perfection; (2) it provides special opportunities for a person to advance towards perfection; (3) that while every human being is obliged to strive to become perfect, not all persons are obliged to take those special and exceptionally effective means that our Lord counselled in the Gospels, that is, absolute poverty, perfect chastity, and obedience; the means that are known as the evangelical counsels; (4) some persons would find it easier to save their soul in the religious state because of its special protections, such as the rule, community life, etc. I may say here that the community life religious live can be of great service to the members by inspiring and encouraging the individual's efforts in the direction of a more intensive love for God; and (5) religious enter upon their chosen and God-given work primarily and immediately *in quest of their own supernatural perfection,* but this in no way lessens, rather it may increase the desire on the part of the religious priest to strive to save the souls of others out of a consuming love for God and His glory.

The vast majority of religious orders are a combination of the contemplative and active ministry. Everywhere one can find religious who are parish priests, chaplains in the armed forces, teachers in schools, colleges and universities, while others are publishers of books, papers and magazines. Those called to the religious priesthood may well find a happy and rewarding combination of the contemplative and the active ministry.

The calling to the diocesan ministry, on the other hand. is quite distinct from that of the calling to the religious life, even though it is quite impossible to appreciate the dignity and glory of a diocesan vocation against the lofty background of the religious state. Msgr. Joseph Clifford Fenton, S.T.D., remarks that "The religious life, even in clerical communities, is geared to produce, as its immediate effect, an increase in personal holiness among those who have the vocation to enter it."

Manifestly, the diocesan priest, like other members of Christ's Church, is invited by God to approach Him through an ever-increasing perfection in the life of charity. While the religious offers full and complete obedience to his competent superior for the purpose of advancing his own progress toward holiness, the diocesan priest is subject to his Bishop for the purpose of his own vocation which is the accomplishment of the sacredotal mission. Diocesan priests of the Western Church are bound to a life of perfect chastity as are those in the religious state. The religious vows perfect chastity in order to rid himself of what might be an encumbrance in a life of perfect devotion, in order to advance in holiness. The diocesan priest is called upon to make this sacrifice in order to further the essential work of the priesthood, to which his life is immediately and completely consecrated. He is privileged to express his love for Christ in giving up all of his life to the holy and cooperative apostolic labor through which the grace of Christ comes to the children of men.

The Most Reverend Wilhelm Stockums, D.D , in his excellent work, "Vocation to the Priesthood," says that "Christ did not institute the priesthood primarily for the

good of the priest himself; He did not establish it *ex pro-
fesso* as a state of personal sanctification or as a means of
such sanctification. In the mind of Christ the priesthood
is an eminently *social vocation,* seeking the good of all,
particularly the supernatural welfare and salvation of mankind. Certainly, no one can doubt but that the priest, like
every other person, must first of all save his own soul. But,
this is not the purpose for which he became a priest; he
became a priest expressly for the purpose of saving the
souls of others . . . A young man who is directing his attention exclusively to his *own* sanctification and to a life of
*personal* piety and virtue, should *not* choose the diocesan
priesthood but should rather knock at the door of a monas-
tery of some contemplative order. Not in the ranks of the
diocesan clergy, but in the cloistered life of a Monastic
community, where he can observe the evangelical counsels,
will the yearnings of his soul be satisfied. There, too, he
will have the opportunity of becoming a priest and of
serving God in sacerdotal piety without being burdened
by the other responsibilities which a diocesan priest takes
upon himself.

"The same applies," continues the Bishop, "to a candidate who desires to become a priest from the motive of
contrition and penance. To him should be pointed out that
the priesthood is not a state specifically intended for the
practice of penance, and that the priest, no matter how
full his life, may occasionally be aware of suffering and
pain, of renunciation and sacrifice, and has not therefore
the primary obligation of leading a penitential life. A
priest's life is fundamentally nothing else than a mediation

of graces and blessings to others. On the other hand, a candidate wishing to do more than the average penance for his past sins and to dedicate the remainder of his life to the special service of God should be told that in the Church are many penitential orders which will gladly open their doors to a sinner, and, in certain circumstances, make it possible for him to enter the priesthood."

Two points from the foregoing must be self-evident, namely, (1) the diocesan ministry is a work a man is privileged and called upon to accept in order to continue and apply the sacerdotal labors of our Lord among His people; (2) the religious life, even in clerical communities, is geared to produce as its immediate effect an increase in personal holiness among those who have the vocation to enter it, but it also, indirectly at least, has the purpose of aiding the ministry of the priesthood, for, all other things being equal, the holier the priest, the more fruitful his ministry.

Anyone who holds that the diocesan priesthood is a sort of "fractional religious life," or that diocesan priests are clerics who have not the courage "to go the whole way" in devoting themselves to Christ, would be particularly guilty of error. Such thinking could only be attributed to a complete misunderstanding of the diversities of the two ministries and functions which go to make up the ordered beauty of operation within the Mystical Body of Christ. Never lose sight of the fact that *both* groups have distinct functions assigned to them within the unity of the Church. They are meant to cooperate with one another. Each must proceed according to its own basic laws and exigencies if it is to do the work which God has assigned to it in the Church. In the existing order of Divine Providence, the continuance of Christ's sacerdotal mission here on earth demands the activity of both groups.

His Eminence Cardinal van Roey published in *Collectanea Mechliniensia* on November, 1952, the following extract from a letter of the Secretariate of State:

"When it is stated that a priest who desires to tend toward perfection ought to become a religious or at least a member of a Secular Institute; and if, to a young man who is hesitating between the secular priesthood and entering religion, one replies that it is a question of generosity; when it is asserted that one who chooses the secular clergy shows that he is not generous enough to give himself entirely to the service of God; when it is felt that a young man who is hesitating as above cannot be advised to enter the seminary rather than a religious institute; if certain persons go so far as to say that the Church "tolerates" the secular clergy as a last resort, but that the ideal would be that all priests be religious — all this represents a false understanding and mistaken application of the Allocution of the Holy Father of 8 December, 1950."

The aforementioned Allocution of His Holiness had as its purpose the clarification of several important questions, one for instance being, "What is the place of the religious clergy in relation to the secular clergy in the constitution which Christ gave to His Church?" The reply was: "If we keep before our eyes the order established by Christ, neither of the two special forms of clerical life holds a prerogative of divine right, since that law singles out neither form, nor gives to either precedence over the other."

Another question concerned the objective reasons for embracing the religious state. The reply to this resolved around the religious state in itself, as a state of perfection which should not, it affirmed, be identified with the vocation of the individual to personal perfection, whether in the "state of perfection" or outside it.

The letter includes this important paragraph: "Consequently it would not be true to say that the secular priest, as regards his personal holiness, is less called to perfection than the religious priest; or that the choice of a secular priestly vocation by a young man is a determination to a lesser perfection than if he had chosen the priesthood in the religious state. It may be that such is the case; it may also be that the choice by the individual of a state other than the state of perfection springs from a greater love of God and a higher spirit of sacrifice than does the choice of the religious life by another. As regards the priest, and the same is true of the candidate for the priesthood, it is not difficult to see that by reason of the dignity of the duties of the priestly function, he too is called in a very special way to personal perfection. This is true even in the case when the one who is endowed with the priestly function is living legitimately in the "state of marriage," as happens in the Oriental rites."

In conclusion then, the letter states, "we must say this: the vocation of the individual to holiness or personal perfection, and the adoption and permanent practice of such perfection, must not be confused with the question of the 'state of perfection' in the juridical sense of the term. The state of perfection is so called and is such because, through the three evangelical counsels, it removes the chief obstacles to the effort toward personal holiness, or to speak more exactly, because it is of its nature suited to keep them out of the way. But, that this state should realize all its potentialities in the life of the individual religious, and so lead effectively to actual holiness, is not assured by the mere fact of having embraced the state of perfection; it depends on the efforts put forth by the subject and the measure in which, in cooperation with the grace of God, he makes the evangelical counsels active in his life."

Having outlined the difference between the diocesan and the religious priest and established the important role each plays in the work of the Church, the question may arise in the mind of some who have little doubt of their call to the priesthood whether or not they must answer the added call to a life in a religious community. Father Sempé, in an article on vocations in the *Dictionnaire de Theologie Catholique,* (t. 15, col. 3155), writes: "A religious vocation does not create an obligation in conscience unless there is a special sign from God, making it obligatory in a given case, or unless the person has so peculiar a character that he needs the religious life for his salvation. Obviously, anyone receiving a vocation would do well to follow it . . . but it cannot be said, as a general rule, that there is a sin in refusing a religious vocation."

Earlier we said that one should use the same means in determining a religious vocation as in determining a vocation to the diocesan priesthood. It might be added here that in both cases the wise thing to do is to talk the matter over frankly with your pastor, confessor, or spiritual director. Miraculous as was St. Paul's conversion, our Lord made use of a human guide to direct him into the priesthood. God taught Ananias what to say to St. Paul, and so, God may enlighten your pastor, confessor or spiritual director regarding your vocation. Canon Law imposes upon priests the duty of promoting vocations, stressing as it does in Canon 1353 that "they should foster in them (boys) the seed of a divine vocation." The Latin text uses the word *germen* — "germ or seed."

There is hardly a diocese in the world which is not suffering a dearth of vocations to the priesthood. Religious orders are likewise handicapped. It would be blasphemous to say that God was withholding what Pope Pius XII called "the impulse and invisible action of the Holy Ghost . . . the divine call," from modern youth, the result of which would be the loss of souls through the lack of priests to carry on His work. As a matter of fact, Pope Pius XI said: "*God Himself liberally sows in the generous hearts of young men this precious seed of vocation.*" The trouble is that not enough young men are willing to accept God's invitation. A great saint and a great educator, St. John Bosco, stoutly maintained that God puts the germ of a vocation into the hearts of at least *one-third* of our young people. If this be true, then, in every class of thirty pupils there should be up to ten vocations. This is a particularly disturbing thought, isn't it? Oh, what a flood of refused calls! What has happened to our youth that God's Will and work mean so little to them? It just could be that the germ of the vocation suffers the same fate the seed suffered in the parable of the sower, as told and explained by our Lord:

"The sower sows the seed . . . and they in whom the word is sown; as they have heard, *Satan* at once comes and takes away the word that has been sown in their hearts." (Mark 4:15).

"And the one sown on rocky ground, that is he who hears the word and receives it immediately with joy; yet he has no root in himself, but continues only for a time, and when trouble and persecution come because of the word, he at once falls away." (Matth. 13:21-22). (This would apply where a person forsakes a true vocation because of parental objections or persecutions). It was our Lord Who said: "He that loveth father or mother more than Me is not worthy of Me." (Matth. 10:37). St. Jerome, writing to Heliodorus, advises him to deal severely with anyone trying to bar his way to the monastic life, even if it should be his own father: "If your father should prostrate himself before you at the door, tread your father down and go on . . . In this case the only way for you to show your affection for your father is to be cruel to him."

"And that which fell among the thorns, these are they who have heard, and as they go their way are choked by the cares and riches and pleasures of life, and their fruit does not ripen." (Luke 8:14).

There, I think, are the answers to the present-day dearth of vocations to the priesthood. Study them well, for therein you may find the reasons for your failing to answer God's call. If this is so, decide now to do something about it.

In endeavoring to solve the problem of a vocation to

the priesthood, the following principles may be of great assistance:

(1) A vocation to the priesthood is not given to all who volunteer to serve. It is given to those whom God calls: "You have not chosen Me," said our Lord, "but I have chosen you." (John 15:16).

(2) A vocation to the priesthood falls under God's ordinary Providence. It is not dealt with by a special or extraordinary Providence which applies to it alone. The ordinary Providence applies to vocation to a state of life, including the married state, the religious state, and the priesthood.

(3) Attraction to the priesthood, whether it be supernatural, voluntary or sensible, is not an absolute proof of a true vocation.

(4) There are certain qualifications which a man must have in order to receive Holy Orders lawfully, yet even these qualities must *not* be regarded formally as signs of a divine decree. They are, however, qualities which the Church considers to be necessary in order that a man may be able to discharge his priestly duties.

(5) No one has a right to expect God to provide a spectacular miracle or sign in order to show him that he is called to the priesthood. The decision is made by the person himself, acting in accordance with the usual laws of supernatural prudence, such as judging objective, external criteria.

(6) The psychological process of choosing the priesthood as a state of life is the same as that employed

in making any other election in life. The act of
choosing a priestly vocation is an act of free election, chosen under the influence of actual graces
as a result of prayer and deliberation.

(7) Before the free election, neither inspiration, revelation, supernatural or natural attraction, nor interior
invitations of the Holy Spirit are necessary in the
soul. All that is necessary for the lawful choice of
the priesthood as a state of life is a right intention
and suitability.

(8) When God chooses one for the priesthood, whether
diocesan or religious, He will, in His infinite power
and wisdom, prepare that subject by bestowing on
him besides what Pope Pius XII called "the impulse and invisible action of the Holy Ghost," such
talents of body and mind as are requisite for such
a calling.

(9) Two elements are essential for a valid and lawful
vocation to the priesthood:
a) a baptized man who has the right intention and
who is canonically suitable for the priesthood,
b) the call to the priesthood produced by the
invitation of the Bishop.

Let us now turn our attention to a consideration of the
positive signs of a vocation to the priesthood.

## CHAPTER FIVE

# THE SIGN OF A VOCATION

From the decree of July 2, 1912, which we quoted earlier in Chapter Four, it is now certain:

(a) that a vocation to the priesthood does not necessarily include any interior inclination of the person or prompting of the Holy Ghost;

(b) that all is required from aspirants to Ordination is a right intention and such fitness of nature and grace, as evidenced in integrity of life, and a sufficiency of learning as will give a well-founded hope of his rightly discharging the obligations of the priesthood; and

(c) that given these conditions, a true vocation is unquestionably conferred by the Bishop at the moment of Ordination.

This *canonical or ecclesiastical vocation* as described in the decree cited above did nothing to rob the *divine vocation* of its signifiicance, and while it placed emphasis on ecclesiastical vocation, it did not by any means intend to belittle or rule out altogether the other form of vocation which takes place by the direct operation of the Holy Ghost.

The ecclesiastical call, which becomes operative by the external expression of the Bishop's will, resulting in the authoritative acceptance of the candidate, is a visible outwardly favorable act, whereas, the divine call is an invisible phenomenon. As for the candidate himself and for his spiritual advisors and for the ecclesiastical authorities, it is very important that these signs of a true vocation antecede the decision of the Bishop.

Here again the decree of 1912 comes to our aid. Although it does not say so explicitly, it sums up everything contained in the o'd familiar concept of certain "signs of a vocation." The decree states that the priestly vocation, and by that it means the divine vocation, consists in those gifts of grace and nature which give rise to the well-grounded hope that the candidate in question will be faithful in the discharge of his priestly duties. His Holiness, Pope Leo XIII, in his Encyclical to the Bishops and Clergy of France on the education of the C'ergy, invites the professors and directors of junior seminaries to "continually study, under the eye and in the light of God, the souls of children and the significant signs of their vocation to the service of the altar."

In the *Rules for the Direction of Education and Discipline in the Seminaries of Italy,* approved by Pope Pius X, it says in Article 86: "Only those students should be admitted to the higher courses who have given *signs* of a vocation to the ecclesiastical state." [1]

(1) "qui indicia praebuerint vocationis ad statum clericalem."

The Sacred Congregation of the Council cites the case of a young man who was dismissed from a seminary "because he did not present the certain signs of a vocation." [2]

Again, notice must be taken of the Code, Canon 1353, in which priests, especially pastors, are urged to guide toward the priesthood "children in whom he notices signs of an ecclesiastical vocation." [3]

Since it appears evident that there are "signs" which would help us decide the possibility of a vocation, the absence of which could nearly always indicate that no vocation to the priesthood exists, it would be well for us to consider the following quite carefully.

In the decision handed down in the decree of 1912 two points were stressed as essential constituents of a vocation to the priesthood: (1) the right intention, and (2) fitness. Let us now consider these in order, beginning with *the right intention.* Three questions come to our minds as we begin to find out what is meant by the right intention as set down by the Commission of Cardinals under Pope Pius X, (1) what it is, (2) what it implies, and (3) what it excludes.

Moral theologians tell us that every moral act must spring from a moral motive, but that this motive need not always be the highest motive, which is love. However, since the higher the goal of an action and the higher the resolve

(2) "eo quod certa vocationis signa non praebeat." Decree: Vetuit (A.S.S., Feb. 1906)

(3) "pueros qui indicia praebeant ecclesiasticae vocationis." Can. 1353

of the will, the loftier the motive must be, in dealing with the priesthood it would seem only reasonable to suppose that the motives would be the highest, or in other words, motives of love: *love for Christ, for His Church, and for one's fellowman.* These three motives aim at the external glory of God, and any one of the three taken individually would constitute such a high degree of right intention that a priestly vocation based upon it would be a satisfactory fulfillment of this important condition for a true vocation.

Whenever one finds a diminishing of the foregoing high motives so that *self* comes to the front and the honor of God is moved to the background, that much is the right intention lessened, so that when one comes to the state where the supernatural sphere is departed from entirely and mere human motives replace them, an adequate intention ceases to exist.

Now, it could be possible that a person might seek the priesthood for his own soul's welfare, thus making his own salvation more secure. Certainly the motive is supernatural, but opinions are divided as to whether such a motive would be adequate to the priesthood. Canon Lahitton holds that such an intention is not adequate. "He who regards," says the Canon, "the priesthood chiefly as a sure means of securing his own salvation does not strive toward it with the right intention." [1] The noted theologian Lehmkuhl maintains a different opinion. Basing his teaching on St. Ignatius, he regards as a criterion of every right choice of vocation, even when the priesthood is being considered,

(1) La Vocation Sacerdotale, No. 430

that "we fix our eyes purely and simply upon the honor of God and our own salvation." [2]

Rather than get into a discussion of these two opinions for they are closer than they seem, it must suffice to say that we must hold that it is a fundamental principle that a person becomes a priest not for himself, but for the honor and glory of God and for the salvation of souls. Now, if the young man who wishes to enter the priesthood to save his own soul knows this principle, and does not let his motive directly exclude every thought of the salvation of others and his motive to provide for the accomplishment of his salvation is to be attained by labors that are directed immediately to the service of God and the promotion of the salvation of others as implicitly required by the acceptance of the priesthood, the right intention could not be considered lacking.

A list of wrong and inadequate motives for seeking the priesthood has been drawn up in an *Instruction* issued by the Congregation of the Sacraments, dated December 27, 1930.

*First*, concerning those of a personal or intrinsic nature we have:

(1) The desire for the more comfortable life of the priesthood, as people often picture it to be,

(2) The opportunity for easy gain,

(3) The desire to avoid manual labor,

(2) Theo-prakt, Quartalschrift, 1914, p. 280.

(4) The prospect of attaining by means of the sacerdotal office a more honorable position, one held in esteem by the world.

*Secondly,* as an external motive (one outside the candidate), the Congregation mentions *grave fear,* whether absolute or relative. This latter includes that reverential fear carried to the extreme that a person would be too fearful and timid to oppose parents who were "pushing" him into the priesthood. Parents have the duty in conscience to refrain from any sort of pressure on their son in his choice of a vocation. Parents who, in spite of this prohibition persist in doing so, according to Canon Law, incur *ipso facto excommunication* if they force their son in any way to take Holy Orders.

God invites but He does not compel. The Church invites but she does not compel: in fact, she exacts a sworn statement in writing from the candidate before ordination, to the effect that he is not being forced to the Order by any sort of compulsion, or by any kind of fear, but rather that he seeks the Order on his own initiative and with perfect freedom.

"I cannot repeat too often," writes Bishop Dupailoup, "that the priesthood in its essence must necessarily be free. All antecedent obligations, all that resembles moral compulsion, and, with far more reason, all that constitutes economic pressure offends in the highest degree against it.

In resumé, therefore, the right intention requisite for a true vocation to the diocesan priesthood includes:

(1) *Love for Christ,* so that the candidate burns with a great desire and yearning to labor for Christ, to

win souls for Him, to make His Kingdom expand
in the souls of men and to dispense His graces
wherever he can.

(2) *Love for His Church,* the teachings of God's
Church and His Sacraments, and a love so intense
that he would be willing to do battle for the
Church and to suffer persecution rather than compromise with evil.

(3) *Love for one's fellow-man* in such a way as to
guide, protect, and save souls; to lead men, women
and children to the heights of virtue and sanctity.
To do this he must never lose sight of the worth
of immortal souls made in the image and likeness
of God. He must realize too what Christ the Redeemer has done and suffered for souls, and lend
himself to God to be His instrument in the salvation of souls.

If these motives are present or attainable, a person
can be considered as having the *right intention* requisite
to the call to the priesthood.

Just as the Church of Christ has definite marks that
arise from her nature and make her recognizable as the
one true Church, so there are certain signs, drawn from
the unique character of the priesthood, which form the
basis on which a genuine God-given vocation can be determined, at least, with human certainty. The first of these
signs is, as we have seen, *a right intention.* The second sign
is the candidate's *fitness,* and fitness consists in such natural and supernatural gifts as will beget the well-founded
hope that the candidate will faithfully discharge all the

duties and responsibilities of the priesthood. Now, what in detail are these gifts of nature and grace? Well, the best authorities list four fundamental qualities: (1) intellectual ability, (2) moral fitness, (3) physical fitness, and (4) a good family background.

(1) *Intellectual ability* implies the capacity to acquire knowledge, and since the ministry is exercised in the intellectual field, it requires intellectual tools. Too, since the priest, because of his office and position, plays a leading role in public life, he therefore must, apart from his purely technical knowledge, strive to acquire a comprehensive general knowledge and culture.

And how will intellectual talent or ability show itself in a candidate for the priesthood? Well, in boyhood, it might show itself in the fact that he can clearly grasp presented scholastic matter and evidence a good memory, willingness to work, steadfast concentration and a persistent and intensive desire for education and culture. When serious failures in studies occur during high school and the student's efforts and achievements in many grades are defective, we may rightly assume that he will not be able to cope with the studies required of him in the seminary.

Ordinarily, no matter how good and pure a boy may be, no matter how faithful he is at receiving the sacraments or serving Mass, if he lacks sufficient intellectual ability, his fitness is essentially defective.

Before quitting this section, let us make a distinction between the *inability to learn* and the *lack of opportunities* for a formal education. It does happen, not infrequently, that due to circumstances, a boy has to leave school to work. The emergency at last passes, and he is free to continue his studies but he may find it difficult to catch up. There are certain seminaries for just such "late vocations", and such a person's pastor would be delighted to make arrangements for an interview with those in charge. If you would rather, you may drop me a letter and I will gladly forward addresses of such seminaries in either the United States or Canada.

.   (2) Moral fitness is a very important requisite for those aspiring to the priesthood. St. Gregory Nazianzen writes: "The priest must first be cleansed before he can cleanse others; he must first himself approach God before he can lead others to Him; he must sanctify himself before he can sanctify others; he must first be himself a light before he can illuminate others." (Apologet. 1). Thus, a boy who is deceitful, dishonest, one who has an habitual predilection for what is indecent; one who lacks special devotion to God and interest in things sacred; one to whom spiritual exercises are boring; and one whose common sense and judgment are constantly poor, such persons ought not aspire to the priesthood.

As to the question of whether one should aspire to the priesthood after having fallen into grave sins against holy purity, we shall let Rev. D. Donnelly, S.J., gave us the answer. "Undoubtedly," writes the priest, "provided that a considerable period (at least one year or more according to the gravity of the falls and the duration of the evil practices) the heart has been pure and the habit conquered." Recent official documents reveal the mind of the Church on the matter relative to those already in semina-

ries. For instance, one such document declares that when
it is discovered that a student has a habit of solitary sin and
has been morally corrupt since youth, especially by
reason of disgraceful relations with adults and persons of
opposite sex, if he has not amended his ways and has not
given consistent and lasting proof of his amendment, v.g.
tested chastity, in proportion that is, to the gravity and
duration of the base habit contracted, which in every case
is not to be less than *at least* a year, he must be dismissed
from the clerical ranks.

His Holiness Pope Pius XI in his encyclical *Ad Catholici
Sacerdotii* of December 20, 1935, declared "those who show
they have a special tendency toward sensuality. . .all these
were not born and are not fit for this sacred office."

It is worthy of note that the Sacred Congregation of
Sacraments set down a general principle in regards to proof
of the virtue of chastity in seminarians and it is as follows:
"A student is well able to stand out chaste and pure if he
is physically and psychologically normal, and, as a result,
is of such a character as to be able to respond to the divine
grace of vocation with full vigor in both physical and psychic orders. To put it briefly, it is very necessary for the
candidate for Orders to have soundness of both soul and
body."

Any one looking toward the priesthood who, after
making use of the ordinary means of prayer and frequenta-
tion of the Sacraments and even of extraordinary means
such as severe penances and abstinences, and in spite of
these has not been able to restrain the vehement stimula-
tions of his base passion or his constitutionally bodily

proneness toward sexual cravings, such a person ought to forsake any idea of the sacerdotal or religious state and confessors and directors of such individuals ought to direct such a decision.

A perusal of the directives of the Sacred Congregation of the Sacraments indicates that those are to be held back from the priesthood who are by nature subject to quite strong propensities to emotion, those of slight constitution with weak bodies, especially those deficient in their nervous system, those prone to sexual degeneracy, and still more, those laboring from stubborn psychic melancholia and dread, or epilepsy, with so-called fixed ideas, or from homosexuality, and those suspected of suffering any mental lesions.

According to Canon Law, a young man whose life and character is marred by grievous and disgraceful defects, especially when they have become public, cannot be placed in the ranks of the priesthood. True, in the past, some great sinners have entered the priesthood but only after they had given ample assurance that they had broken definitely with sin and all sinful habits; profound penance, must have taken place in the past; and their conversion and amendment must be sincere and thorough.

Saint and sinner may present themselves as candidates for the priesthood. Only those are to be held back who will not break with sin or who still carry untamed passions in their hearts.

(3) *Physical fitness.* For centuries the Church has set certain boundaries limiting the acceptance of men to the

priesthood not only from the moral side but from the physical side too. Canon Law deals with these impediments under the heading of irregularities. Canon 984, No. 2, declares irregular only those persons who cannot say Mass "safely, that is, without danger of irreverence to the Sacred Species; or with propriety, that is, without surprise and scandal to the people."

Under bodily defects would come blindness, deafness, muteness, lack of one arm or both arms, lack of one hand or both hands, lack of thumb or index finger; and irregular are the lame, the hunchbacked, dwarfs, lepers, those suffering from venereal disease, those with serious facial defects (lack of nose, ears, lips) and hermaphrodites. With regard to the eyes, the sight of the left, the so-called canonical eye, is important. Since Holy Mass must be said without voluntary oddity and without scandal, such things as excessive nervous trembling and shocking bodily disfigurements would constitute impediments to acceptance into the priesthood. Canon Law expressly states *epilepsy* as a cause of irregularity (Can. 984, No. 3), and permanent mental disorders and diseases.

With the daily advances in medicine, the wonder drugs, and the consummate skill of modern doctors, it may be that some of the aforementioned defects can be corrected. In all matters of health and bodily defects in the irregularities, the Bishop should be consulted and his discretion and judgment followed.

(4) *Family background* and home environment are taken into consideration under the title of *fitness;* in fact, a decree of the Congregation of the Sacraments dated

December 27, 1930, directs that the Church wishes the family circumstances of the candidate for the priesthood to be looked into with an exactness of detail that is very striking.

First, the Church demands that candidates to the priesthood be born in valid Christian marriage. Illegitimacy constitutes a canonical impediment. Two points must be made concerning this: (1) the irregularity is automatically removed by later ecclesiastical legitimation and by solemn religious profession; (2) the Pope may grant a special dispensation when sufficient reasons are present.

Secondly, while the Church is primarily concerned with the candidate's good reputation, she, as the Decree of the Congregation of the Sacraments cited above proves, requests the Bishops to take into consideration, as well, the judgment of public opinion concerning his family. The candidate's family, according to the decree must enjoy a good reputation both from the moral and the religious standpoint.

Our Holy Father teaches us, in general, that God in His all-wise Providence indicates and makes possible to every individual the vocation, whether it be to the priesthood, religious life, Christian virginity in the world, or marriage, which He, in His divine foreknowledge judges most suitable to each one. This becomes even truer in the case of those whom He chooses to be His representatives on earth.

This calling by God is not to be considered as something passive. The truth is that each individual must strive with every energy at his disposal to test his own fitness in the matter. A vocation to a certain state of life is not a matter of fate, nor does it usually result from a directing voice from above.

In the usual course of events three factors are to be considered: (1) the objective possibility of a personal choice of a state in life; (2) the presence of personal fitness and an aptitude for that state of life, and (3) the subjective preference and inclination for a certain state in life.

In the case of one considering the priesthood, if the foregoing triple conditions are fulfilled, and if the Bishop accepts the candidate and admits him to Holy Orders, then the Church has spoken her definitive judgment, and we may assume that, thereby, the divine vocation of the said candidate has been established beyond the need of further testing. There is great strength in the words of the Catechism of the Council of Trent to the effect that "those, however, are said to be called by God who are called by the legitimate ministers of the Church."[1]

(1) Cat. Rom., II, cap. 7, q. 3.

## CHAPTER SIX

## OBSTACLES IN THE WAY...

I have often wondered what St. Mary of Egypt would have said when she was the most sought-after creature in sinful Alexandria, if someone had told her that she would reform her wanton life and go into a desert place and spend forty-seven years in a wilderness without seeing another human face, live on herbs and wild dates, and yet be able to say just before her death that those forty-seven years spent in solitude were the happiest of her whole life? I think she would have said such a person was insane. But the truth is, Mary *did* go into a desert with three loaves of bread that were to last her for years, and she *did* say to Abbot Zozimus just before her death that her heart burned with joy she had never experienced in the midst of the pleasures of Alexandria.

It is surprising, even alarming, to think of the "lame" excuses many young men offer for not accepting God's invitation to them to enter His priesthood. One of these excuses most frequently heard is, "I'm afraid I couldn't endure such a life." When a young man who has a true vocation to the priesthood makes such a statement, he utterly discounts the grace of God. No sooner had St. Mary of Egypt heard a voice say to her as she pressed her sinful lips to a relic of the True Cross and bewailed her sins: "Pass over the Jordan and thou wilt find rest," than she resolved to obey that voice and went into a desert to find a strength she never knew was possible. If God has called you to the priesthood, He will sustain you and help you in ways you could never imagine. Moses thought himself totally inadequate for the task God had chosen for him to perform, and he voiced his fears, to which God replied: "Go therefore, and I will be in thy mouth: and I will teach thee what thou shalt speak." (Exodus 4:12).

To every one God calls to the priesthood, He seems to say: "I will give you a new heart, and put a new spirit within you. . .and will cause you to walk in My Commandments and to keep My judgments and do them." (Ezech. 36: 26-27).

The Council of Trent says: "God commands not impossibilities, but, by commanding, both admonishes thee to do what thou art able, and to pray for what thou are not able (to do), and aids thee that thou mayest be able."

"In the distribution of graces," says St. Cyprian, "the Holy Spirit takes into consideration His own plans and not our caprices."

Another common objection frequently heard is the old chestnut: "I feel I can do more good in the world." Now, no one would dare deny this *if* God wants you in the world. But suppose you are really called to the priesthood? Do you think, under such circumstances, your life in the world would be full and fruitful?

Father Granada said that our true vocation is the main wheel of our entire life. As in a clock or watch, if the main wheel is damaged the entire timepiece is injured; so says St. Gregory Nazianzen, if a person errs in his vocation his whole life will be full of errors: for the state of life to which God has called him will be deprived of the help by which he can, with facility, lead a good life. Amburger puts it this way: "Heavy, indeed, is the responsibility when a person does not listen to the call of the Holy Spirit, or when he casts himself into the turmoil of the world so that the voice of God can no longer be heard."

All objections that arise from futile fear of not being able to put up with burdens of the priesthood ought to be banished from your mind. "God," writes St. Thomas, "does not destine men to such and such a vocation without favoring them with the gifts at the same time, and preparing them in such a way as to render them capable of fulfilling the duties of their vocation, for, says St. Paul: 'Our sufficiency is from God, who also hath made us fit ministers of the New Testament'"(2 Cor. 3:5).

The main question here is not the doing of good alone, but of doing the *most* good, and doing the most good where God wants you to do it.

Sadly enough, another objection frequently heard these days is: "My parents are against my going to the seminary." Incredible as it seems, this objection is a real one, and one that is most confusing to a Catholic boy who has heretofore looked to his parents for spiritual guidance. What actually is behind such an objection? Well, this sort of thing is a form of selfishness on the part of the parents, and oddly enough, in not a few cases, born of a misplaced concern for the happiness of their offspring.

The selfish parents usually put on the same sort of fireworks when their teen-age sons and daughters talk of getting married. No matter who the future husband or wife-to-be is, the reaction is the same. "He or she is not the right person for you." If your parents object to your entering the seminary, two to one they would want to pick your future wife. The point is, they want you to stay home, they want you still to be their "little boy." If you should marry, they are the type who would want to turn the second floor into an apartment for you and your bride. Selfish parents will do a job on you no matter what your vocation is.

The other reason why some parents do not want their son to be a priest is because they want him to be happy, and happiness to them is all wrapped up in a home, a family car, a T.V., and white collar job in the city. Celibacy they can't understand, and to them all it means is that it is a source of frustration and unhappiness. Confidentially, I often think some parents object to their son's going to the seminary or novitiate simply because they fear he will find out a little later that he has no vocation, and they don't want the stigma of "ex-seminarian" hanging around the neck of their boy or touching them. This is all pretty crazy. Boys who try and then leave the seminary are double heroes, heroes in leaving all to follow Christ, and heroes again dropping out when it is learned that it is God's will that they live in the world. The parents of the Little Flower both tried religious life, found out it was not God's will, and returned to the world to raise a family, one of whom became a saint.

Pope Pius XI, in his Encyclical "The Catholic Priesthood," addressed these memorable words of warning to selfish and worldly-minded parents: *Yet it must be confessed with sadness that only too often parents seem to be unab'e to resign themselves to the priestly or religious vocations of their children. Such parents have no scruple in opposing the divine call with objections of all kinds; they even have recourse to means which can imperil not only the vocation of a more perfect state, but also the very conscience and the eternal salvation of those souls they ought to hold so dear. This happens all too often in the case of parents who glory in being sincerely Christian and Catholic, especially in the higher and more cultured classes.*

*This is a deplorable abuse, similar to that unfortunately prevalent in centuries past, of forcing children into the ecclesiastical career without the fitness of a vocation. It hardly does honor to those higher classes of society, which are on the whole so scantily represented in the ranks of the clergy. The lack of vocations in families of the middle and upper classes may be partly explained by the dissipations of modern life, the seductions, which especially in the larger cities, prematurely awaken the passions of youth; the schools in many places which scarcely conduce to the development of vocations. Nevertheless, it must be admitted that such a scarcity reveals a deplorable falling off of faith, in the families themselves. Did they indeed look at things in the light of faith, what greater dignity could Christian parents desire for their sons, what ministry more noble, than that which, as We have said, is worthy of the veneration of men and angels? A long and sad experience has shown that a vocation betrayed — the word is not to be thought too strong — is a source of tears not only for the sons but also for the ill-advised parents; and God grant that such tears be not so long delayed as to become eternal tears."*

God once tried Abraham's faith by asking him to sacrifice his beloved son Isaac. God, too, may want to test the strength of your vocation by permitting your parents to violently object to your becoming a priest. You may have to risk the fury of your parents in carrying out your decision, but do it anyway. Remember our Lord's words: "He that loveth father or mother more than Me is not worthy of Me." (Matth. 10: 37).

Once your vocation to the priesthood becomes evident, turn every energy toward the goal. There may be obstacles, there may be disheartening discouragements to beset you on the way, but never lose sight of the goal and the rewards promised to you by a God Who is ever faithful to His promises.

It would appear that our Lord often deigned to keep the promise of special rewards for discipleship ever before His Apostles. For instance, there was the time our Lord went through Samaria to Sichar, to the site of Jacob's Well, on a mission to save one soul, known only to us in Holy Scripture as "the Samaritan Woman." Arriving at the well, our Lord sent the Apostles on into the city for food, and

He sat patiently at the well awaiting a certain woman to come to draw water. Sure enough, the woman did come, and our Lord opened the conversation by placing Himself in the position of asking of her a favor, for He said, "Give Me to drink."

Amazed that a Jew would deign to speak to a Samaitan, much less ask for a favor, the woman was greatly confused. Our Lord seized upon this opportunity to speak of a "living water" which He could give, which if anyone would drink, he would never thirst again, saying, "the water that I will give him shall become in him a fountain of water, springing up into life everlasting." (John 4:14).

We all know how Christ revealed His knowledge of her sinful past, her five husbands, how He revealed His Messiahship to her, and how, at the return of the Apostles to our Lord at the well, the woman left her water-pot behind her and went into the city proclaiming to all of the people she met: "Come, and see a man who has told me all that I have ever done." (John 4:39).

In the meantime the Apostles begged our Lord to partake of the food they had procured, and He answered: "I have food to eat which you do not know . . . My food is to do the Will of Him Who sent Me, to accomplish His work." (John 4:34).

Then, our Lord seized upon the occasion to speak to the Apostles about zeal for the salvation of souls. "Do you not say," Christ remarked, " 'there are yet four months, and then comes the harvest.'? Well, I say to you, lift up your eyes, and behold that the fields are already white for the harvest." (Was there ever such an appeal for missionaries?)

Then, as a strengthening motive, Christ deigned to remind them of the eternal rewards for such an endeavor in these words: "And he who reaps, receives a wage and gathers fruit unto life everlasting, so that the sower and the reaper may rejoice together." (John 4:35, 36).

The lessons Christ taught at Jacob's Well are stupendous. First, there was His zeal. You see, Christ could have taken four roads to reach Galilee. Three of them skirted Samaria, the fourth went right through it. The difficulty in taking the fourth road lay in the fact that our Lord would have to walk up a veritable mountain to reach Sichar. That was the road the Master chose. It was in the noonday sun that He reached the city of Jacob's Well, tired and thirsty, but He counted every inconvenience insignificant, if He could save a soul. Priests must be likewise inspired with a great zeal for souls. St. Bernard reminds us that "in the eyes of God a soul is more valuable than the whole world." And "Why," asks St. Leo, "should you take the honor of the priesthood if you labor not for the salvation of souls?"

*Secondly*, there was a lesson of tenderness and concern for the feelings of the Samaritan sinner woman. This He demonstrated by dispatching the Apostles on an errand so that the woman would not be embarrassed at having to admit to wrong-doing in the presence of others.

*Thirdly*, our Lord demonstrated at Jacob's Well that He can reveal heavenly secrets to the most unlikely persons, and use such persons to bring others to Him. Scripture tells us that the Samaritan woman went into the city and related all that she had seen and heard, and the townspeople "went therefore out of the city and came unto Him . . . Now of that city many of the Samaritans believed in Him, for the word of the woman giving testimony . . . So when the Samaritans were come to Him, they besought Him to stay there; and He stayed two days." (John 4:40).

*Fourthly,* the Samaritan woman left her water-pot behind at the well when she departed to tell her townspeople of her encounter with the Messias. That forgotten waterpot will ever be the symbol of those who would be other Christs. No one, you see, ever comes to Christ without having to leave something behind: sins, a former way of life, parents, friends, or worldly possessions.

*Fifthly,* there was the great lesson our Lord taught His disciples concerning His zeal for the complete accomplishment of His Father's will. He who loves the Will of God enjoys continual peace even in this life. But we must remember that our merit consists in embracing the Divine Will, not so much in things that are pleasing to us, as in those that are opposed to self-love. In these we show the strength of the love we bear God. If it is God's Will that you should be a priest, follow that will, if you would enjoy peace even in this life.

*Sixthly,* there was the broad invitation to consider the magnitude of the work of converting pagan nations that are "white already to the harvest." St. Patrick was called to such a task and he accepted the challenge. Oddly enough, St. Patrick was the only example of an individual who brought the Gospel to a pagan nation and lived long enough to see that whole nation converted.

*Finally,* there was the reward. It seems that our Lord felt it was necessary to keep the idea of a reward before those whom He had invited to be His followers. At Jacob's Well that day He mentioned it again. Referring to the harvest of souls, He said: *"He who reaps receives a wage and gathers fruits unto life everlasting."* (John 4:36).

When the road to the priesthood seems particularly rough, and when once attained, continues to be narrow and up-hill, keep these words ever before you: *"He who reaps receives a wage, and gathers fruit unto life everlasting."*

So much for so little! So very much!